Memoirs on Pauperism and Other Writings

MEMOIRS ON
PAUPERISM

— AND OTHER WRITINGS —

Poverty, Public Welfare, and Inequality

ALEXIS DE TOCQUEVILLE

Edited and translated by

CHRISTINE DUNN HENDERSON

University of Notre Dame Press
Notre Dame, Indiana

University of Notre Dame Press
Notre Dame, Indiana 46556
undpress.nd.edu

Copyright © 2021 by University of Notre Dame

Published in the United States of America

Library of Congress Control Number: 2020950374

ISBN: 978-0-268-10904-2 (Hardback)
ISBN: 978-0-268-10905-9 (Paperback)
ISBN: 978-0-268-10907-3 (WebPDF)
ISBN: 978-0-268-10906-6 (Epub)

CONTENTS

ACKNOWLEDGMENTS

Many people contributed—either directly or indirectly—to the creation of this volume, and I am indebted to them all. Lenore Thomas Ealy first suggested that "someone" should translate the *Second Memoir on Pauperism*, and both the introduction and the *Second Memoir* benefited from her deft editing and keen ear for language. Other early encouragement for working on the memoirs came from the late John Blundell and from Steve Wrinn at University of Notre Dame Press. I am also grateful for the feedback from the several groups with whom I have shared discussions of the memoirs over the years: attendees at a 2013 dinner colloquy entitled "The End of Social Justice" sponsored by The Philanthropic Enterprise; students and faculty at Furman University in 2014, and a group brought together by the Bastiat Society in Indianapolis that same year; my former colleagues at Liberty Fund; and the participants in a 2019 colloquium sponsored by the Mercatus Center (with the support of the John Templeton Foundation).

Hank Clark, Enrico Colombatto, and Catherine Labio read drafts of the various translations and offered many suggestions for improvement. I am indebted to them for generously sharing their time and expertise and for saving me from countless blunders. I am similarly indebted to the anonymous readers at University of Notre Dame Press for their close readings of this book and for their many helpful suggestions about the introduction and the translation itself. Despite the heroic efforts of all of these people, I am sure some translation errors remain; responsibility for these lies entirely with me. Finally, Chandran Kukathas read every word of this book, offering support, insightful comments, and bad puns along the way. James Henderson provided equally strong moral support and slightly better puns. Both of these proto-Tocquevillians have enriched my life beyond words; I dedicate this volume to them.

A NOTE ON THE TEXTS

These translations are based on the French editions of Tocqueville's texts as found in the multivolume *Oeuvres Complètes* (OC) published by Gallimard, under the direction of François Mélonio. Both *Mémoires* and the *Lettre sur le paupérisme en Normandie* are found in *Mélanges* (OC, vol. 16), while "Paupérisme en Amérique" is an appendix to *Du système pénitentiaire aux États-Unis, et de son application en France* and is found in the OC, volume 4. As noted, all references to *Democracy in America* are from the historical-critical edition of *Democracy in America*, edited by Eduardo Nolla, translated by James T. Schleifer, and published by Liberty Fund (2010).

Notes that are original to Tocqueville are indicated with superscript letters and appear at the bottom of the page; editorial notes are indicated with superscript numerals and appear at the back of the book. Unless otherwise noted, all italics in the text reflect italics in the French sources.

INTRODUCTION

Christine Dunn Henderson

Alexis de Tocqueville (1805–59) is best remembered in the United States for *Democracy in America*, his penetrating study of life in the early nineteenth century. Tocqueville was, of course, an analyst of his own France, and his *The Old Regime and the Revolution* remains a classic analysis of prerevolutionary and revolutionary France. Less well known, however, is that Tocqueville was also keenly interested in England, traveling there several times and following with great attention the political and social developments there during his lifetime. One outgrowth of his interest in England's politics was his *Memoir on Pauperism*, a brief but powerful piece written following an 1833 visit to England and delivered to the Royal Academic Society of Cherbourg in 1835. This memoir, which was not included in the early editions of Tocqueville's collected works and which was not even translated into English until 1968, captures England at a very specific moment, as her Elizabethan-era poor laws were undergoing major revision, via the Poor Law Amendment Act of 1834.[1]

In the *Memoir*, Tocqueville explores the unanticipated evils arising from public assistance programs; via this investigation, we can glimpse some of Tocqueville's influences, as well as the distinctiveness of his analysis of democracy — an analysis that remains constant across his thought and that connects the *Memoir* to his other works. In terms of influences, his exploration of how public charity causes the ranks of paupers to swell is shaped by the work of J.-B. Say, and the account of man's movement from the state of nature to civil society is clearly indebted to Rousseau. In terms of continuities with Tocqueville's other works, the *Memoir*'s discussions of the links between poverty and crime recall similar themes explored in "Pauperism in America," an appendix to the 1833 *Penitentiary Report* (coauthored with Gustave de Beaumont), which had provided the original "excuse" (as Tocqueville described it) for the trip to the United States that eventually spurred the writing of *Democracy in America*. Echoes of some of *Democracy in America*'s central elements can also be found in the *Memoir*, particularly in the importance ascribed to voluntary associations in a free society, in Tocqueville's preference for local action, and even in the elements of democratic psychology at play in the statement of the problem as well as in potential solutions.

The *Memoir* ends with the promise of a sequel, in which Tocqueville would outline solutions to the discrepancies between the intentions and outcomes of policy he observed in England. Although he partially drafted a *Second Memoir on Pauperism*, that work remained unfinished, the problem of crafting an improved remedy unsolved. This volume brings the two memoirs together for the first time in English, along with a letter fragment considering pauperism in Normandy, and the "Pauperism in America" appendix to the *Penitentiary Report*. When read in combination, the *Memoir*, its unfinished sequel, and the other pieces invite exploration of several themes, including the challenge of poverty in modern society, the possibilities and difficulties associated with various attempts to find solutions, and the manner in which democratic society—the inevitable future in Tocqueville's view, as well as the "operative idea" behind his thinking—affects both the issue of poverty and various solutions to it. This introduction focuses primarily on the two memoirs, exploring the problems of modern poverty as well as the various solutions Tocqueville ponders, particularly considering them in the context of the themes developed more fully in *Democracy in America*.

SOME BACKGROUND

Before we turn to the memoirs themselves, a brief overview of the status of poor relief in England and Wales is necessary. Until the mid-sixteenth century, aid to the poor had generally been administered by the church, on a parish-based level. When Henry VIII began expropriating England's monasteries in 1536, however, two effects were soon felt that caused assistance to the poor to move out of the hands of the church and into the hands of the state: on the one hand, the church had fewer resources to allocate to its poor-relief efforts, and on the other hand, the state's coffers expanded. The state thus began to fill the vacuum left by the expropriated monasteries and to provide relief and assistance to the poor. This activity was codified in a series of laws enacted during the reign of Elizabeth I, the best known of which was the Poor Law Relief Act of 1601, also known as the Elizabethan Poor Law.[2] In essence, the Poor Law created a national system of relief for the poor, who were divided into "able-bodied" poor, who were capable of working, and the "impotent" poor, who were not. Shelter was provided to both groups, and the impotent poor—usually the aged or infirm—were given additional relief in the form of money, food, or clothing. As a condition of assistance, the able-bodied poor were required to work either outdoors or in workhouses. Relief was financed through local land taxes and administered by local parishes, whose overseers could at least theoretically claim to possess knowledge of each recipient's circumstances and character.[3]

This system remained in place for almost two hundred years, with the only major reform being the 1795 establishment of the

Speenhamland System, which provided bread subsidies to "every poor and industrious man" whose wages fell below a certain level, as well as bread subsidies based on the number of children in a family. While well intentioned, the Speenhamland System had unanticipated and undesirable consequences, for the bread subsidy kept wages artificially low—sometimes to the point that working seemed less advantageous than collecting benefits—while the increased subsidy for additional children was widely viewed as encouraging poor families to have children they could not afford, thus swelling the ranks of eventual paupers.[4] In Gertrude Himmelfarb's analysis, the Speenhamland System created a "cycle of evils," while Karl Polanyi states simply, "In the long run the result was ghastly."[5]

Tocqueville penned the first *Memoir* as the poor laws of England and Wales were being reformed again, through the 1834 Poor Law Amendment Act, whose chief architect was Tocqueville's friend and correspondent, the lawyer and economist Nassau Senior. The reformed law eliminated subsidies to the able-bodied poor, made the terms of workhouse employment less favorable than employment that was not state-sponsored, and required unmarried mothers to name their child's father if they wished to receive subsidies for the child. The Act also created a national commission to oversee and coordinate relief efforts, yet the commission's powers were limited, and while it could recommend that parishes undertake certain relief actions (e.g., build new workhouses or make improvements in existing ones), it could not compel parishes to follow its recommendations.

THE *MEMOIR ON PAUPERISM*: A TALE OF THREE PARADOXES

In typically Tocquevillian manner, the *Memoir on Pauperism* is structured around three paradoxes, whose elaborations allow

Tocqueville to develop his critiques of state-based aid programs. The first is quite simple: England, which is Europe's wealthiest country, also has the greatest number of paupers, or claimants of public assistance. Fully one-sixth of England's population depended upon public charity when Tocqueville was writing, whereas in less developed countries with lower standards of living, significantly fewer people turned to the state for assistance. Probing the causes of this paradox, Tocqueville offers an account of man's movement from the state of nature into civil society, which is heavily indebted to Jean-Jacques Rousseau and which reads like a summary of Rousseau's *Discourse on the Origin of Inequality*, with its highlighting of the development and growth of "artificial inequalities" among human beings. The emphasis in the *Memoir*'s history is on inequality, and at first blush, it stands in some contrast to the movement of time sketched in *Democracy in America*, in which history is cast as the spread of equality of conditions.[6] In the *Memoir*, equality seems to characterize only history's first and final eras, with inequality dominating the entire middle period, perhaps reaching its apex with feudalism. The most recognizable feature of feudalism is the hierarchical relationship between its members,[7] but it is also characterized by smaller societies whose members have reciprocal duties and responsibilities.

The end of feudalism—and with it, small societies in which lords would be responsible for care for the poor—was accompanied by the growth of industrialism; in Tocqueville's account, these elements worked together to increase England's pauperism. He offers a detailed explanation of how both the peasants and the nobles contributed to urban and industrial expansion. On the one hand, the peasants' proximity to the wealthier lord gradually exposed them to the greater luxuries the lord possessed. Perhaps because of the spread of the idea of equality Tocqueville traces in the preface to *Democracy in America*, peasants eventually began to desire the lord's luxuries they had seen (i.e., peasants saw themselves as equal enough to possess them, too); in order to have such luxuries, peasants abandoned the subsistence-level income they earned through farming and became industrial workers. As peasants left the land in hopes of earning (and spending) more, the production of nonessential goods increased; consequently, more workers were needed to manufacture those goods, and more peasants left the land to meet this labor demand. On the other hand, demand also rose from the side of the nobles, in that they constantly wanted to improve their condition by acquiring increasingly refined and more luxurious goods.

Thus, peasants were progressively motivated to leave the land, to move to larger villages and cities, and to engage in the manufacturing and trade of luxury—or nonessential—goods. Tocqueville calls this an "immutable" law governing the advance of civilization; he broadly describes these developments in terms of progress and advance. Yet this advance was not without costs, and in fact, Tocqueville saw this very progress as both the direct and indirect source of the increased pauperism he observed in modern England.

The most straightforward relationship between these developments and the rise of those seeking poverty relief is that poor persons who abandon agricultural labor to work in the production of luxury goods increase their exposure to the risks of fortune, because the products of their labor are nonessential. Thus, not only do they no longer produce foodstuffs that would allow them to sustain themselves in difficult times, but if demand for their products vanishes, their market and means for survival disappear. This is one clear source of pauperism: displaced industrial workers whose products are no longer desired and who, through lack of skills or simply lack of positions, cannot find work in the production or sales of whatever goods are in demand and who therefore turn to the state for assistance. Here, Tocqueville assumes a static view of the economy, and he misses something important that he captures in *Democracy in America*: the dynamism of a democratic society—extending to a dynamic economy, in which people retrain and find new jobs, or invent new products to meet new market demand.

In his analysis of America, this dynamism is the positive side of democracy's motion,[8] yet it is absent—perhaps because 1830s England was less democratic than 1830s America?—from his analysis of England.

A second, less obvious source of pauperism exists, one that sheds light on human psychology and how equality shapes notions of justice. Again probably following Rousseau, Tocqueville displays an awareness that human desires are potentially infinite and that, as economic conditions improve over time, desires for material goods and comforts expand; such desires come, moreover, to be viewed as "needs" to the point that in a developed economy "the lack of a multitude of things causes poverty," whereas a less developed society understands poverty simply as the lack of essentials such as food or shelter.[9] Tocqueville's awareness of how wants become needs is very astute, and he offers valuable commentary on today's equality debates as well as on why equality seems to have become the primary good in contemporary democratic societies. In other writings, Tocqueville raises the question of whether this psychology becomes more acute as equality spreads and as the less well-off come to see themselves as fundamentally the same as the more affluent. In *Democracy in America*, for example, he notes that the first passion to which equality gives rise is the love of equality, and with that, the hatred of any inequalities. Or, as he puts the same idea in *Democracy in America*'s "three races" chapter: "There is, moreover, a singular principle of relative justice that is found very deeply buried in the human heart. Men are struck much more by the inequality that exists within the interior of the same class than by the inequalities that are noticed among different classes."[10]

Ironically, then, the prosperity and success of early industrial England led to an increase in the numbers of paupers, both because a developed economy (in Tocqueville's view) exposes increased numbers to fortune and because nonessentials become viewed as "needs," thus prompting the have-nots to make claims for public assistance in order to secure these "necessities." This expanding view of "necessities" is, however, not confined to the "have-nots"; it is shared by an overwhelming majority, cutting across class and economic lines. In the Tocquevillian analysis, all strata of society come to believe individuals are entitled to more than a subsistence standard of living, and eventually, society "believes it must come to the aid of those who are deprived of them [nonessentials], and it cures evils that it did not previously even perceive."[11] All of these elements work together to produce the rise in England's pauperism, and as Tocqueville presents it, there is a certain inescapability to this process. Human beings turning to their fellow human beings for material assistance seems all but inevitable; if this is indeed the case, the question becomes how best to cope with swelling demands for assistance.

Two options for providing poverty assistance present themselves—private charity and public charity; via their comparison and contrast, Tocqueville is able to articulate and explore the *Memoir*'s other two paradoxes. He begins by noting that private charity, which "leads each individual to relieve, according to his means, all of the ills that are found within his reach," is a natural impulse, presumably a manifestation of human sympathy or our instinctive concern and feeling for our fellow beings. Public charity, on the other hand, is a constructed and modern form, one that is "less instinctive, more rational, less enthusiastic," and that "leads society . . . to attend systematically to the relief" of its members' sufferings.[12] In the context of relief to the poor, the second type of charity assumes the form of government-sponsored public assistance programs, and although Tocqueville is ultimately critical of these programs' unintended consequences, he is quick to note the appeal of the idea of public charity, or the appeal of social programs more generally. In an analysis that might also explain the attraction of ideas such as "social justice," Tocqueville writes,

> At first sight, there is no idea that appears more beautiful and more grand than public charity.
>
> Society reflects upon itself, daily probing its injuries and concerning itself with healing them; while assuring the rich of the enjoyment of their goods and protecting the poor from the excess of their misery, society also demands from some a portion of their superfluity in order to provide necessities for the others. This is certainly a grand spectacle. . . .[13]

Yet the beauty of this vision is illusory or fleeting at best. Public charity, by contrast, is not fleeting, and Tocqueville notes the irony that England's prosperity has allowed her to create public charities to "help," but these public charities are ultimately more harmful than helpful. In Tocqueville's view, public charity has transformed assistance from a temporary to a permanent measure; by doing this, public charity has also transformed the poor into a permanent underclass. This is the *Memoir*'s second paradox: that unlike other rights, which elevate their possessor, the right to public charity degrades its possessor.

The Second Paradox

Tocqueville is generally an admirer of rights, asserting in *Democracy in America* that "the idea of rights is nothing more than the idea of virtue introduced to the political world."[14] Rights exist in a suprapolitical context, as the principles to which oppressed minorities can appeal, above an otherwise omnipotent majority. The *Memoir* echoes this praise of rights, asserting that "in general, there is nothing that elevates and sustains the human mind more than the idea of rights."[15] But if the idea of rights is generally elevating, Tocqueville believes the practice of one particular type of right—the right to public charity—is degrading, and he offers an analysis of what he sees as the "fatal consequences" of public assistance programs.

The same questions of unintended consequences and moral hazard that animate today's debates about public assistance programs lie at the heart of Tocqueville's critique of public charity, which begins with an examination of the effects of public charity on the work ethic. Contra the standard Lockean mode emphasizing human industriousness, Tocqueville believes that necessity is the ordinary motive for work and that only a very few individuals work because they desire to improve their own condition. Man is, in Tocqueville's view, essentially lazy and shortsighted— not interested in working and not interested in saving or accumulating.[16] Far from being natural, then, industriousness is largely a product of necessity, and so is the work ethic. This view of human nature is important in the context of public charities, because their creation of a right to financial assistance to all who have need and their expansion of that right to cover more than the most basic of necessities actually remove the need to work that is present when subsistence is on the line. With the genuine need of subsistence provided for, most individuals' incentives to work and to save are destroyed.

The erosion of the work ethic is one of the unintended consequences resulting from the creation of public assistance programs. Another unplanned consequence is due to the very nature of such large-scale programs, for they are institutional and law based, which means they are also impartial or "blind" in important senses. An advantage of this kind of impartiality is that recipients do not have to curry favor with donors and recipients are not turned away for reasons not related to desert. Yet there is also a drawback, because an impartial law does not and cannot differentiate between those who work (but who might still require subsidies) and those who choose not to work. Thus—and again, based on Tocqueville's psychology—there is no moral high ground to claim by working rather than receiving a subsidy, and there is also a decreased motivation to support oneself rather than taking public assistance.

Tocqueville asserts that by disincentivizing the poor from working and by destigmatizing the receipt of charity or welfare, public assistance laws actually discourage poor persons from making efforts to improve their condition and to find new employment. Tocqueville believes that this produces despair and eventually depression in unemployed individuals, thus further diminishing their likelihood of trying to find employment. In addition to these psychological effects, Tocqueville finds (and his belief is based on courtroom testimony he witnessed and recorded while in England) that by encouraging idleness, the Poor Law's assistance programs breed a host of vices, including criminality and moral turpitude; poverty relief enshrined in law, he writes in the selection from the *Penitentiary Report* included in this volume, will "always deprave the population that it is designed to assist."[17] He is especially concerned about effects that the destigmatization of illegitimacy and unwed motherhood will have on mores.

That Tocqueville is concerned with the condition of mores comes as no surprise, given the pivotal role played by mores in supporting laws and preserving a free society. What might be surprising, though, is what the *Memoir* suggests about the relationship between mores and laws. Usually, Tocqueville casts this relationship with mores as the dominant factor, more powerful than laws. Statements such as "I am persuaded that the most fortunate situation and the best laws cannot maintain a constitution without mores" reflect this belief, which Tocqueville saw as a "central point" in his own thought. But he also acknowledged a reciprocal influence between the two, in which mores modify laws, but laws also modify mores.[18] The *Memoir* gives evidence of this second direction of influence, with the argument that the legal destigmatization of accepting public assistance or having illegitimate children will eventually be accompanied by a general moral (in the sense of "related to mores") and social destigmatization of these things.

Certainly, some of Tocqueville's worries about the effects of simple entitlements could be alleviated if the law required claimants to perform public work as a condition of their receipt of benefits. Tocqueville believes this would be the best solution to the moral and social problems with which he is so concerned, but he is also alert to a host of logistical difficulties involved with implementing such a requirement. He particularly expresses worries about the coordination problem of trying to match the "public workers" (paupers, laboring as the condition of their receipt of benefits) to the number of public projects in a given region. With a surplus of paupers in a region, the temptation would be to create make-work projects in that region. With more projects than paupers, it might be expected that paupers would relocate to areas needing workers, but the Settlement Act, which was not repealed until the passage of the Poor Law Amendment Act in 1834, placed restrictions on paupers' freedom of movement. Although some of Tocqueville's concerns about coordination and some of his questions about freedom of movement could, perhaps, be obviated by making assistance programs entirely coordinated and administered at the national level, Tocqueville's repeated preference for local action over national action and his belief that the absence of centralization is an important element in preserving liberty prevent him from endorsing national programs.[19]

Coordination and centralization issues aside, Tocqueville is alert to another difficulty that would continue to exist under a centralized system and that might become even more problematic there. This difficulty is the growth of a bureaucracy to "manage" and coordinate programs. He is especially scornful of public assistance bureaucrats, calling them "an idle and lazy class, living at the expense of the industrial and working class."[20] His primary concern, however, is that the industrious members of society will be resentful of both the nonworking, permanent recipients of public assistance and those bureaucrats who earn their livings by overseeing the transfer of wealth from the more industrious (or fortunate) to those who are less so. This resentment, he fears, poses a significant threat to social cohesion and harmony, as well as to political stability.

The Third Paradox

Tocqueville's concerns about the effects of "public alms" on social cohesion bring him to the *Memoir*'s final paradox, which is that although private charity appears inferior to public charity, it is actually superior and more effective. Public charity, as he notes in the beginning of the *Memoir*, initially appears to be an improvement upon older forms of charity, because it regularizes and extends the earlier forms, in which one individual gave assistance directly to one or more of his fellow citizens. Public charity thus seems an advance, because it broadens traditional charity's scope to cover a wider group and because it provides a more dependable and systematic solution to the problem of poverty. Yet Tocqueville sees the comparison between public and private charity differently, asserting that private charity is better for the individual recipient, the individual donor, and society as a whole.

Tocqueville observes that in asking for private charity, the poor man "recognizes . . . his inferior state" in relation to his fellow citizens, but he believes that the poor man views that inferiority as limited to the economic realm and as a temporary condition.[21] Tocqueville suggests that the applicant for state charity, by contrast, experiences humiliation in having to publicly acknowledge his "inferiority" or his failure to be able to provide for himself and his family. He fears that such admissions will demoralize the claimant, thus furthering the demoralization he has described in the early portions of the *Memoir*.

His additional worries are that the poor man's humiliation will make him resentful at having to make a public application for assistance, as well as envious of those who possess greater wealth than he.

Tocqueville also fears that public assistance programs might create resentment in the opposite direction and that the wealthy might come to resent the poor to whom public relief—relief funded through taxes levied on the wealthy—is given. Because funding for public charities is compulsory (via taxation) and because the individual "donors" have no personal connection to the recipients, Tocqueville believes the wealthy person is likely to resent the recipient of public alms and to see him as "only a greedy stranger, summoned by the legislator to share his goods."[22] Mutual resentment is thus liable to develop, and the social consequences of this are fatal. Tocqueville warns, "Far from tending to unite into a single people these two rival nations that are called the rich and the poor and that have existed since the beginning of the world, legal charity breaks the only line that could have been established between them" and "readies them for combat."[23]

Private charity, by contrast, creates none of these problems, and rather than separating wealthy and poor into resentful and envious classes, private charity produces genuine connections across two classes who might otherwise be hostile to each other. Tocqueville argues that private charity unites the wealthy and the poor because the act of giving personally involves the donor in the fate of the individual whose condition the donor has undertaken to ameliorate. Such personal involvement presumably develops the sympathy that had weakened with the end of feudalism. In the context of the ideas developed in *Democracy in America*, Tocqueville's approbation of such bonds between individuals might be thought of as an example of the rich associative life that is characteristic of American democracy. For Tocqueville, associative life is "the mother science," one that creates connections among citizens and teaches them to assist each other, rather than turning to the government for help. The science of associations is essential for preserving a free political life in a modern world in which individualism produces isolation and atomization.[24]

THE *SECOND MEMOIR*: NEW SOLUTIONS OR AN INTRACTABLE PROBLEM?

Having thoroughly exposed what he sees as the evils of public charity, Tocqueville is left with the challenge of finding a better alternative. He does not reject public assistance entirely: in the *Memoir* and other writings, he endorses permanent public assistance for certain categories of people (the aged, the infirm, the ill, the insane). He also approves of temporary public assistance during emergency situations, as well as publicly funded "free schools" for the children of the poor.[25] Ultimately, Tocqueville seems to concede that the scope and character of modern life—greater anonymity, fewer ties among individuals, and the increased exposure of workers to fortune[26]—render some form of public assistance necessary.

The question then becomes what form of public assistance programs would be best (or least bad). Having offered such a penetrating analysis of the problems associated with public assistance programs, however, Tocqueville seems to have painted himself into a corner, in terms of finding alternative arrangements. The *Memoir* ends with the promise of a sequel, in which alternatives would be proposed, but Tocqueville never delivered a second installment. His notebooks, however, include an unfinished *Second Memoir on Pauperism* that was drafted in 1837, revealing that he continued to wrestle with the problem, considering different options at different moments, but never settling upon any solution or set of solutions.

Shifting his focus to France in the *Second Memoir*, Tocqueville weighs a variety of possibilities for avoiding policies likely to generate more pauperism. Taking note that French laborers were still found more in agriculture than industry, he considers solutions such as the expansion of the opportunities for rural individuals to acquire small pieces of land and for urban workers to acquire shares in the factories in which they labor.

Tocqueville seems to have felt that if agricultural workers owned the land they worked and if factory laborers were shareholders in the factories that employed them, their means of employment and incomes would be more secure, less subject to fortune. The *Memoir* details the insecurities to which Tocqueville thought modern industrial workers were exposed, and although Tocqueville believed that modern agricultural life was certainly less exposed to risk than modern industrial life, he also saw that the modern land laborer was more precariously placed than his ancestor had been. Two reasons account for the loss of "job security" in the agricultural sector. The first is that the concentration of land into larger parcels—while itself facilitating improvement in agricultural processes and, thus, in agricultural production— had made possible greater mechanization, which could diminish the number of agricultural laborers required to work a given amount of land.

Second, Tocqueville feared that the shift from small landowner to paid laborer on a larger tract of land could leave the individual unemployed and without prospects for supporting himself if the landowner decided to convert farmland to pasture. One of the reasons for which Tocqueville advocates property ownership, then, is that it would give the agricultural laborer greater control over his own fate.

Another advantage of property ownership seems to be the cultivation of certain character traits and certain habits. Mores, perhaps the most powerful force for shaping political and social society, are defined broadly by Tocqueville, to include all of the ideas, opinions, and habits of the heart within a society. As we have seen, the corruption of good mores is one of the most dangerous consequences of public charities or entitlement programs.[27] Ownership, argues Tocqueville, fosters good mores, because it encourages the agrarian virtues such as industriousness and prudence, and habits of "order, activity, and economy."[28] By contrast, the individual who owns no property feels himself constantly exposed to chance and at the mercy of others. This, in turn, erodes his feelings of self-reliance, independence, and responsibility. Tocqueville attributes the "beast-like heedlessness for tomorrow" he finds among England's peasants and industrial laborers to a certain corruption of their mores, and he believes this corruption has contributed to increased pauperism among both rural and urban populations. In addition to providing people with more stable means of providing for themselves, then, expanding the class of those who own at least part of the enterprise from which they earn their living would combat this moral corruption; it would thus combat the rise of pauperism on two fronts.

In Tocqueville's view, however, economic uncertainty and instability are unavoidable aspects of the modern condition. Ownership of land and partial ownership of factories by workers might diminish the percentage of the population exposed to fortune, and they could help instill habits essential to economic independence—as would the "agricultural colonies" Tocqueville mentions in "Pauperism in America"—but these would likely only be partial solutions.[29] Tocqueville ultimately believes that poverty is an inescapable feature of the modern world and that the need for some forms of mutual assistance cannot be eliminated. Yet he also believes that the older type of private charity (individual to individual) is no longer a sufficient solution to the poverty characterizing the modern world; a more regularized system is necessary for a world in which needy individuals and possible donors lack connections to each other via local associative life.

The *Second Memoir* explores one possibility for creating a private yet institutionalized form of charity, a possibility

Tocqueville believes would improve both upon existing forms of public charity and upon less regularized forms of traditional private charity. This is the savings bank, or savings society. As described in the *Second Memoir*, part of the savings bank's function is identical to that of a traditional savings bank, in that workers and peasants would be able to make small deposits, which would earn interest and gradually accumulate. Savings banks were abundant in the France of Tocqueville's day, but they were administered by the state, which guaranteed depositors returns of a certain percentage. The *Second Memoir* endorses encouraging workers and peasants to save in savings banks, yet it is critical of the existing French system, particularly of the risks that offering such guaranteed returns might pose to the state's financial security.

Tocqueville prefers that the savings banks be run at a local level and that they be reformed to a kind of a hybrid between a voluntary charity and a traditional savings bank. The hybrid bank/charity he has in mind is something like the *mont-de-piété*, which originated in fifteenth-century Italy and which allowed needy individuals to borrow funds at low interest. The terms of the loan from a *mont-de-piété* were generally favorable to the borrower, rather than the lender, and the capital from which loans were made came from various sources, including revenues from public fines as well as contributions from wealthy donors and possibly even corporations. Donors contributed to the *mont-de-piété* simply as an act of philanthropy, and they did not expect to see a return on their contributions.

Understood from the donors' perspective, the reformed savings banks are a form of voluntary association. That Tocqueville would turn to local, voluntary associations as a possible solution (and that he would prefer them to a variety of state-centric alternatives) is not surprising, given the centrality of local action and voluntary associations in *Democracy in America*.[30] As we have already seen, both decentralization and associative life are key to the preservation of democratic freedom, because both serve as counterweights to the feelings of isolation and weakness Tocqueville saw as among the greatest dangers to liberty in an age of equality.

A FOURTH PARADOX?

Tocqueville scholar Seymour Drescher suggests that Tocqueville was writing the *Second Memoir* in 1837 but left it unfinished as he took up the challenge of completing volume 2 of *Democracy in America* (1840). It is in this volume of *Democracy in America* that Tocqueville reflected most seriously on the problems of soft despotism and the relationship between voluntary associations and government in democratic societies.

Tocqueville's observation that local and voluntary associations would provide the most appropriate approach to solving social problems did not resolve his concerns about the tendencies toward centralization in democracies. Moreover, his advocacy of local and associative provision of poverty assistance did not allay his misgivings about the social impact of industrialization, which he saw as having the tendency to concentrate resources in commercial enterprises and thus increasingly to expose both capital and labor to the hazards of fortune. We can see these tensions emerging clearly in the reflections on pauperism in both the *Memoir* and the *Second Memoir*.

Reading the memoirs alongside *Democracy in America* raises another question about the relationship between these problems and possible remedies in Tocqueville's thought more broadly. The "problem" of the rise of pauperism as he sees it is multifold. To the extent that increased need for charitable assistance is a function of the greater uncertainty characterizing the modern industrial worker's life, Tocqueville believes that growth in the number of people needing financial assistance to survive is inevitable.[31] Moreover, the older "solution" of aristocrats providing alms for the poor who lived on their lands is impossible, both because of the demise of the aristocracy (both in France in particular and in democratic society more generally) and because modern life is more anonymous and fluid. In Tocqueville's view, then, the advance of equality has at least two downsides when viewed from the perspective of the problem of poverty. One is the destruction of a code that obliged the wealthy to care for the poor in their locality, and the other is the rise of urban and industrial centers, in which people lack traditional social connections to each other. Tocqueville suggests that voluntary associations would have to supply connections among individuals, and this is what he means when he says, "Associations, among democratic peoples, must take the place of the powerful individuals that equality of conditions has made disappear."[32] Hence, in the "Letter on Pauperism in Normandy," Tocqueville proposes solving the problem of rising poverty by creating local and regional voluntary associations dedicated to poor relief. Such private associations, he believes, would serve as surrogates in the modern age for magnanimous individuals of the past, and he hopes that these new associations would avoid the pitfalls of public welfare, while also combining the advantages of private charity with the greater efficiency and reach required in the modern era.

The art of association is the art of empowerment, of allowing individuals to feel their collective strength and to understand that they can solve their own problems without turning to government.[33] Tocqueville fears that without learning to associate—to help each other—they will "fall into impotence," neither able to help themselves nor able to interest their fellows in providing assistance.[34] Under such circumstances, the state becomes the only solution, for only it is powerful enough to accomplish goals that appear too vast for individuals who believe themselves weak and who do not understand the possibilities of voluntary associations. Should the state come to the rescue, however, the door opens to the soft despotism Tocqueville so worries will endanger liberty by enervating souls and keeping citizens in perpetual childhood, "liberating" them from the burden of making their own choices, until they are no longer capable of exercising their freedom at all.

Thus, the "fourth paradox" is really more of a question—and a fairly simple one at that: Is the slide into soft despotism inevitable? In the Toquevillian analysis, democracy can generate feelings of weakness and isolation, which would cause individuals to turn to government, rather than each other, to solve social problems such as poverty. Doing this creates even more feelings of weakness, isolation, and impotence, until the very idea of associating to solve their own problems is impossible. Yet the solution Tocqueville offers to the problems of democratic isolation and impotence is precisely what democracy makes so problematic: turning to each other. In one sense, this is very Tocquevillian and very in keeping with Tocquevillian arguments such as that the best remedy to the dangers of liberty is more liberty. But in another, it is more complicated, for once a people has begun to turn to government to solve its problems—as had happened in England well before Tocqueville penned the *Memoir*—it is not clear that this slide into soft despotism can be reversed. But perhaps it can be slowed, and certainly, encouraging voluntary associations and other nongovernmental solutions to social problems would slow that slide.

In the *Second Memoir* Tocqueville wonders briefly whether industrial workers' associations might obviate the need for excessive concentrations of capital, but he dismisses this solution as not yet ripe. Desiring voluntary and local solutions, Tocqueville concedes that some form of governmental assistance to the poor seems necessary in the modern world and possibly—in the cases of free schools for children of the poor, for example—even desirable. Private initiative might be stronger and more effective than public initiative theoretically, but once poverty relief begins to be a governmental task (as Tocqueville believes it inevitably will), can it ever be returned to private hands? Skeptics from a modern public choice perspective, echoing Tocqueville's observation of the tensions here, would remind us that agencies have their own interests, and once empowered, agencies would be reluctant to return their powers to private associations or even to diminish the sphere of their own jurisdiction. In the *Memoir*, Tocqueville acknowledges something of this issue in his criticisms of bureaucrats and in his discussions about the coordination problems associated with public relief efforts. But the deeper Tocquevillian concerns about whether the movement to governmental solutions can be reversed, I think, are the psychological ones about whether a people that has begun voluntarily to cede its liberty—and has begun the slide into soft despotism—can ever reclaim it.

Tocqueville does not directly address the question of whether soft despotism can be reversed by reinvigorating citizens' desires to take care of themselves and to find private solutions to social problems. Indeed, *Democracy in America*'s rather bleak ending, in which Tocqueville warns of the dangers soft despotism poses to liberty, suggests that a reversal might not be possible and that once people begin to turn to public agents to find solutions to problems such as poverty, their abilities to find their own solutions will be gravely and irrevocably weakened. Yet two moments in *Democracy in America* suggest that reversing the descent into soft despotism might be possible. The first comes in the discussion of how free institutions and local political participation combat what Tocqueville sees as the harmful effects of individualism.[35] Tocqueville believes the exercise of political rights constantly reminds the individual of his connections to his fellow citizens and of the fact that "the duty as well as the interest of men is to make themselves useful to their fellows." Political participation might originally be motivated by interest or feelings of duty, but over time, the activity of promoting the general interest becomes habitual and eventually a consciously sought end, both within a political context and beyond that context. Describing this process, Tocqueville writes, "You first get involved in the general interest by necessity, and then by choice; what was calculation becomes instinct; and by working for the good of your fellow citizens, you finally acquire the habit and taste of serving them."[36]

The second moment comes just pages later, in Tocqueville's discussion of the importance of civil associations. There, he warns of the dangers of "social power"—later explicitly identified as government—sapping individuals' ability to solve their problems without its assistance. He writes, "The more it puts itself in the place of associations, the more individuals, losing the idea of association, will need it to come to their aid." Again, only the practice of associative life can halt this process, and in the discussion that follows, Tocqueville makes clear that the practice of associative life can also reverse the process, restoring independence and initiative where they have been lost. He states, "Sentiments and ideas are *renewed*, the heart grows larger, and the human mind develops only by the reciprocal action of men on each other" (emphasis added).[37] Thus, perhaps it is possible to turn the tide and to renew citizens' desire and ability to find private solutions to their problems. But Tocqueville is explicit that government cannot legislate this process of reinvigorating citizen initiative. He writes, "It does not depend on the laws to revive beliefs that are fading."[38] Government cannot legislate this civic renewal, but it can and should act indirectly, by awakening our natural instincts to help each other. In the context of poverty relief, government can encourage and strengthen what Tocqueville considers a natural sentiment to provide assistance to the needy, but it can do this only by stepping back and allowing individuals to fill the vacuum and to find their own responses to this problem.

In the *Second Memoir*, Tocqueville had begun to think about how economic empowerment through land ownership and personal savings might help protect people from the exposure to chance in a world dominated by manufacturing economies and the production of luxury goods. Against the problems set out in *Democracy in America*, we can consider how economic responsibility might also assist in the development of the capacity of social action by individuals and voluntary associations. Today, we should not read Tocqueville's memoirs on pauperism as failures in their inability to offer blueprints for a solution; rather, we can approach them as invitations to us to reengage in thinking about these issues and about how to find creative, new solutions to what Tocqueville observed was a characteristic tension between liberty and equality in the modern world.

MEMOIR ON PAUPERISM

(1835)

FIRST PART
On the Progressive Development of *Pauperism* in the Modern
Era and the Methods Used to Combat It

When one surveys the diverse countries of Europe, one is struck
by a most extraordinary and apparently inexplicable sight.[1]

The countries that appear the poorest are those which, in reality, contain the fewest indigents, while among the peoples
whose opulence you admire, one part of the population is obliged
to rely upon the gifts of the other in order to live.

Travel through England's countryside, and you will believe
yourself transported into the Eden of modern civilization. With
roads magnificently maintained, clean and new houses, well-fed
herds wandering in rich meadows, strong and healthy farmers,
wealth more dazzling than in any country in the world, more or-
nate and exquisite basic comforts, there is everywhere the feeling
of order, of well-being, and of leisure; a feeling of universal prosperity that seems to exude from the atmosphere itself and that

thrills the heart with every step. This is how England appears at the traveler's first glance.

Now go more deeply into the interior of the villages,[2] examine the parish registers, and you will discover with an indescribable shock that one-sixth of the inhabitants of this flourishing kingdom live at the expense of public charity.

If you turn your gaze to Spain, and above all to Portugal, an entirely different sight strikes your eyes. Everywhere in your path, you will encounter a poorly fed, ill clothed, ignorant and coarse populace, living in miserable homes in the midst of half-uncultivated countryside. Nevertheless, the number of indigents is insignificant in Portugal. M. de Villeneuve estimates that one pauper is found for every twenty-five inhabitants of this kingdom.[3] The celebrated geographer Balbi had previously given the figure of one indigent for every ninety-eight inhabitants.[4]

Rather than comparing two foreign countries to each other, contrast diverse parts of the same empire, and you will arrive at a similar result: you will see proportionate growth of, on the one hand, the number of those living in comfort, and on the other hand, the number of those who fall back upon public donations in order to live.

According to the calculations of a conscientious writer[a] whose other theories I am, in fact, far from approving, the average number of indigents in France is one pauper per twenty inhabitants. But we can see immense differences among different parts of the kingdom. The department of the Nord, which is certainly the richest, the most populous, and the most advanced in everything, counts close to a sixth of its population for whom the assistance of charity is necessary. In the Creuse, the poorest and the least industrialized of our departments, we only meet one indigent for every fifty-eight inhabitants. By these statistics, the Manche is shown as having one pauper for every twenty-six inhabitants.[5]

---

a. M. de Villeneuve.

I think it is not impossible to give a reasonable explanation for this phenomenon. The effect to which I have just called attention comes from many general causes that would be too time-consuming to detail here, but they can at least be indicated.

Here, in order to make myself better understood, I feel the need to return for a moment to the beginning of human societies. I will then rapidly go down the river of humanity to today.

Behold men gathering for the first time. They come out of the forest, they are still wild,[6] they join forces not to enjoy life, but to find the means of surviving. Shelter against the intemperance of the seasons, sufficient food—such is the object of their efforts. Their minds[7] do not go beyond these goods, and if they obtain them without trouble, they judge themselves satisfied with their fate and doze in idle comfort. I have lived in the midst of barbarous tribes in North America; I have lamented their destiny, but they do not find it at all cruel. Sunk in the middle of the smoke of his hut, covered in coarse clothes which are the work of his hands or the fruit of his hunting, the Indian looks with pity at our arts and considers the advances of our civilization a tiresome and shameful subjugation; he envies us only our weapons.

Having reached this first age of societies, men thus still have very few desires and hardly feel any needs other than those felt by animals; through social organization, they have only discovered the means of satisfying them with less effort. Until they become acquainted with agriculture, they live by hunting; from the moment they learn the art of making the earth bring forth harvest, they become farmers. So each works the field that has fallen to him to bring forth whatever could nourish him and his children. Land ownership is created, and with that, the most active element of progress is born.

From the moment men possess land, they settle down. In cultivating the earth, they find abundant resources against hunger. Assured of survival, they begin to glimpse that human existence offers other sources of pleasures beyond the satisfaction of life's first and most urgent needs.

As long as men had been wanderers and hunters, permanent inequality had not been able to insert itself permanently among them. There was no outward sign at all that could permanently establish the superiority of one man and, above all, of one family over another family or another man; and had this outward sign existed, it would not have been transferrable to his children. But as soon as land ownership was known and men had converted vast forests into arable fields and grassy meadows, from then on, we saw individuals gathering into their hands much more land than was necessary to feed themselves and thus perpetuating ownership in their descendants' hands. From then on, superfluity exists; with superfluity is born the taste for pleasures other than the satisfaction of the most basic physical needs.

It is at this stage of societies that the origin of almost all aristocracies must be found.

While some men already know the art of concentrating all the material and intellectual enjoyments of life with wealth and power in the hands of the few, the half-civilized crowd [*la foule à demi-sauvage*] still ignores the secret of spreading comfort and liberty to all. At this epoch of the history of the human species, men have already abandoned the crude and proud virtues that had been born in the forests; they have lost barbarism's advantages without acquiring those of civilization. Attached to the cultivation of the soil as if it were their only resource, they disregard the art of defending the fruits of their labors. Placed between the wild independence they are no longer able to desire and the civil and political liberty that they do not yet understand, they are given over to violence and deceit without any appeal, and they reveal themselves ready to submit to every tyranny, provided that they are left to live—or better yet, to vegetate—near their fields.

It is thus that landed property is accumulated immoderately and that government becomes concentrated in a few hands. It is thus that war, rather than imperiling the people's political condition as is the case nowadays, menaces the individual property of each citizen. Inequality reaches its furthest limits in the world and one sees the spirit of conquest, which has been the father and mother of all aristocratic societies, spread.

The barbarians who invaded the Roman Empire at the end of the fourth century were savages [*sauvages*] who had glimpsed landed property's utility and had wanted to get its advantages for themselves. Most of the Roman provinces that they attacked were peopled by men who had long been dependent on farming and whose mores[8] had been softened by the peaceful activities of field labor but for whom civilization had not yet made sufficient progress to make them capable of fighting against the primitive fierceness of their enemies. Victory placed not only the government but also the property of the third estate[9] into the barbarians' hands. The farmer became a tenant farmer. Inequality passed into laws, and from having been a fact, it became a right. Feudal society was organized and the Middle Ages were born. If we pay attention to what has happened since the birth of societies, we will easily discover that equality is only found at the two ends of society. Savages are equal because they are all equally weak and ignorant. Very civilized men are able to all become equal because they all have similar means of attaining comfort and happiness at their disposal. Between these two extremes, the inequality of conditions is found: the wealth, enlightenment, and power of some and the poverty, ignorance, and weakness of all the others.

Able and wise writers have already worked to make the Middle Ages known; others—among whom we are able to include the secretary of the Academic Society of Cherbourg[10]—are still working on this. I thus leave this great task to men more capable of completing it than I; here, I only want to examine one corner of the immense picture that the feudal centuries unfold before our eyes.

In the twelfth century, that which has since been called the third estate did not yet exist. The population was divided into only two categories: on the one side, those who cultivated the soil without possessing it, and on the other, those who possessed the soil without cultivating it.

As for the first group of the population, I imagine that their fate was in some respects less to be pitied than that of the common people nowadays. These people, who had more liberty, elevation, and morality than our colonies' slaves, nevertheless found themselves in an analogous situation. Their means of survival were almost always guaranteed; in this, the master's interest coincided with theirs. Limited in their desires as well as in their power, without distress about the present, tranquil about a future that was not in their control, they enjoyed that type of vegetative happiness whose charm is as difficult for the highly civilized man to understand as its existence is difficult for him to deny.

The other class presented the opposite picture. There is found the custom of hereditary leisure as well as assured superabundance. I am far from believing, however, that even in the midst of this privileged class, the search for life's pleasures pushed as far as is generally assumed. Luxury can easily exist in the midst of a nation that is still half-barbarous, but comfort cannot. Comfort presupposes a large class whose members are simultaneously employed in trying to make life sweeter and more comfortable. Now, in the period about which I am speaking, the number of those who were not exclusively preoccupied with the cares of survival was very small. This group's existence was brilliant and lavish, but not commodious. They ate with their fingers from plates of silver or engraved steel; their clothes were covered with ermine and gold, and undergarments were unknown; they lived in palaces whose walls were covered with dampness, and they sat on ornately sculpted wooden seats near immense hearths in which entire trees were consumed without any spread of warmth. I am convinced that there is not a provincial town today whose comfortable inhabitants do not have more true conveniences of life in their homes and who do not find it easier to satisfy the thousand needs to which civilization has given birth than did the proudest baron of the Middle Ages.

If we turn our gaze to the feudal centuries, we will thus discover that the great majority of the population lived almost without needs and that the remainder experienced only a few. The land was enough, as it were, for all. Comfort was found nowhere, survival everywhere.

It was necessary to establish this point of departure in order to make what I am going to say well understood.

As time goes on, the population that cultivates the soil conceives of new tastes. Satisfying the most basic needs is no longer enough. The peasant, without leaving his fields, wants to find himself better lodged, better clad; he glimpses the pleasures of comfort and wants to acquire them. On the other side, the class that lives off the land without cultivating the soil expands the sphere of its pleasures; its enjoyments are less lavish, but more complicated and varied. A thousand needs that were unknown to the medieval nobles spur on their descendants. A large number of men who live on and from the soil leave the fields and find a way to provide for their livelihoods by working to satisfy these new needs that arise. Agriculture, which was everyone's occupation, is now only that of the many. Next to those who live from the products of the earth, but do not work, arises a numerous class that lives by its own industry,[11] but not by working the land.

As each century slips from the Creator's hands, the human mind is developed, the circle of thought broadens, desires increase, and man's power grows. The poor and the rich, each in their sphere, develop ideas of new pleasures that their predecessors had overlooked. In order to satisfy these new needs, which could not be satisfied by the cultivation of the earth, a portion of the population leaves field work each year to devote themselves to industry.

If we carefully consider what has happened in Europe over the past several centuries, we are left convinced that as civilization has progressed, a vast displacement of population has taken place. Men left the plow for the shuttle and the hammer; from the cottage, they went to the factory. In so proceeding, they obeyed the immutable laws governing the growth of organized societies. Thus, we can no more assign a term to this movement than we can impose limits upon human perfectibility. The limits of both are only known to God.

What has been and what is the consequence of this gradual and irresistible movement we have just described?

An immense quantity of new goods has been introduced into the world; the class that remained in agriculture has found at its disposal a host of pleasures that the preceding century had not known. The farmer's life has become easier and more comfortable; the great proprietor's life has become more varied and more ornamented. Comfort is found within reach of the many, but these happy outcomes have not been achieved without a necessary cost.

I said that in the Middle Ages comfort was nowhere, survival everywhere. This summarizes in advance what will follow. When almost all of the population lived by cultivating the soil, extreme poverty and coarse mores were found, but man's most pressing needs were met. It is very rare that the earth cannot at least supply that which appeases the call of hunger's cry to one who waters the earth with his sweat. The population was poor indeed,[12] but it survived. Today, the population is happier, but there is always a minority ready to die of want if it did not have recourse to public support.

Such a result is easy to understand. The farmer produces basic foodstuffs. Their sale might be more or less profitable, but it is more or less guaranteed; and if an accidental cause prevents the selling of agricultural products, these products at least furnish the means of life to those who have harvested them and allow them to wait for better times.

By contrast, the worker speculates on artificial and secondary needs that can be limited by a thousand causes and can be completely eliminated by great events.

Whatever might be the hardships of the times, or the high costs or cheapness of commodities, each man needs a certain amount of nourishment or he languishes and dies, and one may trust that he will always make extraordinary sacrifices in order to obtain them. But unhappy circumstances can lead people to deny themselves certain pleasures in which they had effortlessly indulged in other times. Yet it is the taste for and use of these pleasures upon which the worker counts in order to live. If they are lacking, he has no other resource. His own harvest is burned, his fields are made barren, and if by any chance such a situation continues, he sees only dreadful poverty and death.

I have only spoken of the case in which the population limits its needs. Many other causes can lead to the same effect: excessive production by citizens, foreign competition . . .[13]

The industrial class that so powerfully helps the well-being of others is thus much more exposed than they are to sudden and incurable evils. In the great fabric of human societies, I consider the industrial class as having received from God the special and dangerous mission of providing, by its own risks and dangers, the material happiness of all the others. Now, this natural and irreversible movement of civilization tends to increase continually the relative size of those who belong to this class. Each year, needs multiply and diversify, and with them grows the number of individuals who hope to create comfort by working to satisfy these new needs rather than staying employed in agriculture: this is a major subject of reflection for today's statesmen!

This is the principal cause to which we must attribute what happens within wealthy societies, where comfort and indigence encounter each other to a greater extent than elsewhere. The industrial class, which supplies pleasures of the greatest number, is itself exposed to miseries that would be almost unknown if this class did not exist.

However, still other causes contribute to the gradual development of pauperism.

Man is born with needs and he makes needs for himself. Those of his physical constitution are primary; secondary are those of habit and education. I have shown that at the origins of societies, men have hardly any but natural needs, seeking only to live; but as life's pleasures become more expansive, men acquired the habit of indulging in some of those pleasures, which end up becoming almost as necessary as life itself. I will cite the habit of using tobacco because tobacco is a luxury good that has spread all the way to the wilderness and has created among the natives [*sauvages*] an artificial pleasure that must be obtained at any price. Tobacco is almost as indispensable to the Indians as food; they are as inclined to appeal to their peers' charity when they lack one as when they lack the other. Thus, it is one cause of begging that was unknown to their forefathers.

What I have said about tobacco applies to a multitude of objects that one could not do without in civilized life. The more a society is wealthy, industrious, prosperous, the more the pleasures of the greatest number become varied and permanent, the more that they become, through habit and example, real needs. Civilized man is thus infinitely more exposed to the vicissitudes of fate than is savage[14] man. That which never happens to the second, except from time to time and in certain circumstances, can always and under very ordinary circumstances happen to the first. Along with the circle of his pleasures, he has expanded the circle of his needs, and he more greatly exposes himself to the blows of Fortune. From this comes the fact that the poor of England seem almost rich to the poor of France, who seem rich to the indigents of Spain. What the Englishman lacks has never been possessed by the Frenchman. And it is like this as one continues down the social scale. Among very civilized peoples, the lack of a multitude of things causes poverty; in the savage state, impoverishment consists only in not finding something to eat.

Civilization's progress not only exposes men to many new miseries; it even brings society to relieve miseries of which, in a half-civilized country, one does not even dream. In a country where the majority is poorly clad, poorly housed, poorly fed, who thinks of giving clean clothing, healthy food, and comfortable lodging to the poor? Among the English, where the greatest number, possessing all of these goods, sees not being able to enjoy them as a terrible misfortune, society believes it must come to the aid of those who are deprived of them, and it cures evils that it did not previously even perceive.

In England, the average of pleasures for which a man can hope in life is higher than in any other country in the world. This drastically facilitates the spread of pauperism in that kingdom.

If all of these reflections are correct, one will easily see that the more nations are wealthy, the more the number of those who appeal to public charity must multiply, because two very powerful causes tend toward this result: among these nations, the class most naturally exposed to need is increasing incessantly, and on the other side, needs themselves infinitely multiply and diversify; the opportunity of finding oneself exposed to some of them becomes more frequent each day.

We should not give ourselves over to dangerous illusions; let us look calmly and peacefully at the future of modern societies. Let us not become drunk by the spectacle of its greatness; let us not become discouraged by the sight of its miseries. As civilization's present movement continues, we will see the pleasures of the greatest number grow; society will become more perfected, wiser; existence will be more comfortable, sweeter, more embellished, longer. But at the same time, let us foresee that the number of those who will need to turn to the support of their fellow men in order to receive a tiny part of those goods will continually grow. This double movement can be slowed; particular circumstances among different peoples will precipitate or pause its course; but no one can stop it. Let us therefore hasten to look for the means of attenuating the inevitable evils which are already easy to foresee.

SECOND PART

There are two types of beneficence: one leads each individual to relieve, according to his means, all of the ills that are found within his reach. This type is as old as the world; it began with human miseries. Christianity made it a divine virtue and called it charity.

The other, less instinctive, more rational, less enthusiastic, and often more powerful, leads society itself to concern itself with the misfortunes of its members and to attend systematically to the relief of their distress. This was born out of Protestantism and is developed only in modern societies.

The first is a private virtue; it escapes social action. The second, by contrast, is produced and regularized by society. It is therefore with the second that we must especially be concerned.

At first sight, there is no idea that appears more beautiful and more grand than public charity.

Society reflects upon itself, daily probing its injuries and concerning itself with healing them; while assuring the rich of the enjoyment of their goods and protecting the poor from the excess of their misery, society also demands from some a portion of their superfluity in order to provide necessities for the others. This is certainly a grand spectacle in the presence of which the mind is elevated and the soul cannot fail to be touched.

How is it that experience comes to destroy a part of these beautiful illusions?

England is the only country in Europe that has systemized and broadly applied these theories of public charity. Under Henry VIII, during the religious revolution that changed the face of England, almost all of the charitable communities were suppressed, and because the goods of these communities passed into the hands of the nobles and were not at all divided among the hands of the people, it followed that the number of poor then existing stayed the same, while the means of providing for their needs were partly destroyed. The number of poor thus grew significantly. Struck by the offensive sight of the people's miseries, Elizabeth, Henry the VIII's daughter, considered substituting an annual subsidy furnished by the local villages for the alms that the suppression of the convents had so greatly reduced.

A law promulgated in the forty-third year of that queen's reign[b] provided that in each parish, inspectors of the poor would be named and that these inspectors would have the right to tax inhabitants in order to feed the disabled indigents and furnish the others with work. As time marched forward, England was increasingly led to adopt the principle of legal charity. Pauperism grew more rapidly in Great Britain than everywhere else. Some general causes and others unique to that country produced this sad result. In civilized life, the English were ahead of the other nations of Europe; all of the reflections I have previous offered are thus particularly applicable to them, but there are others that apply to them alone.

England's industrial class provides for the needs and the pleasures of not only the English people but also of a large part of humanity. Its well-being or its miseries depend not only on what happens in Great Britain but also in some sense on all that happens under the sun. When an inhabitant of the Indies reduces his expenses and cuts back his consumption, there is an English manufacturer who suffers. England is thus the country in the world in which the farmer is most strongly attracted to industrial work—but also finds himself the most exposed to the vicissitudes of fortune.

For a century, something has been happening among the English that could be considered extraordinary if one paid attention

---

b. See, first, Blackstone, book 1, chapter 4; second, the principal results of the inquiry made in 1833 into the state of the poor, contained in the book entitled *Extracts from the Information Received by His Majesty's Commissioners as to the Administration and Operation of the Poor-Laws*; third, *The Report of the Poor-Laws Commissioners*; fourth and finally, the law of 1834 that has been the result of all of these studies.

to the spectacle provided by the rest of the world. For a hundred years, landed property has been divided up in the known world; in England, it has been continually concentrating. Midsized plots of land have disappeared in vast holdings; large-scale farming has replaced small-scale farming. There could be some not uninteresting explanations of this to offer, but they would draw me away from my subject; the fact suffices and it is constant. The result of this is that, while the farmer is drawn by his own interest to quit the plough and enter into the factories, he is in some way pushed by the consolidation of landed property to do it despite himself. This is because, proportionately speaking, infinitely fewer workers are needed to cultivate a large estate than a small field. The earth fails him and industry calls him. This double movement pulls at him. Of the twenty-five million inhabitants peopling Great Britain, no more than nine million are involved with cultivating the soil; fourteen [million] or almost two-thirds follow the risky opportunities of commerce and industry.[c] Pauperism thus necessarily grew faster in England than in countries whose civilization had been equal that of the English. Once having accepted the principle of legal charity, England was not able to depart from it. Thus, the English legislation about the poor was nothing but a long development, over two hundred years, of Elizabeth's laws. Almost two and a half centuries have passed since the principle of legal charity was fully accepted by our neighbors, and we can now judge the fatal consequences that have followed from the adoption of this principle. Let us examine them one by one.

With the poor person having an absolute right to society's assistance and finding in all places a public administration organized to furnish him with it, we quickly see the rebirth and spread across a Protestant country of those abuses for which

---

c. In France, the industrial class is still only one-quarter of the population.

the Reformation had rightly reproached some of the Catholic countries. Man, like all composite beings, has a natural passion for idleness. Yet there are two motives that impel him to work: the need to live and the desire to improve his living conditions. Experience has proven that most men can be sufficiently motivated to work by only the first of these motives, and that the second is powerful only among a small number. Now, a charitable organization, open indiscriminately to all of those who are in need, or a law that gives to all poor—whatever the origin of their poverty—a right to public assistance, weakens or destroys the first stimulant and leaves only the second intact. Whether English or Spanish, the peasant who does not feel the intense desire to improve the condition in which he was born and to leave that sphere (a weak desire that in most men collapses easily)—I say that the citizen of both these countries has no interest in working, or if he works, he has no interest in saving. He thus remains idle or thoughtlessly spends the precious fruits of his labors. In either of these countries, different causes bring the same result: it is the most generous, active, and industrious part of the nation that devotes its assistance to furnishing the means of life to those who do nothing or who make bad use of their work.

We are certainly far from the beautiful and seductive theory that I set out above. Is it possible to escape these disastrous consequences of a good principle? For myself, I confess that I consider them inevitable.

Here, one might interrupt me by saying: "You assume that assistance will be given to poverty, whatever its cause; you add that public assistance will take away the obligation to work among the poor; but this is to state as a fact something that remains to be proven. What prevents society from inquiring into the causes of need before giving assistance? Why wouldn't work be imposed as a condition upon the able-bodied indigent who appealed to public sympathy?" I respond that the English laws have developed the idea of these palliatives, but they have failed, and this can easily be understood.

Nothing is as difficult as distinguishing the nuances that separate an undeserved unhappiness from misfortune that vice has produced. How many miseries are simultaneously the result of both of these two causes! What profound knowledge of the character of each man and of the circumstances in which he has lived is presupposed by judgment about such a point; what enlightenment, what certain discernment, what cold and inexorable reason! Where will be found the magistrate with the conscience, the time, the talent, the means of devoting himself to such an examination? Who will dare to let a poor man die of hunger because this death is his own fault? Who will hear his cries and argue about his vices? At the sight of the miseries of our fellow men, even personal interest is quieted. Would the interest of the public treasury be more powerful? And if these emotions, which are beautiful even when they are misplaced, will not reach the soul of the overseer of the poor,[15] will not fear reach it instead? Holding in his hands the sorrows or the joys, the life or the death of a considerable portion of his fellow men—of the most disordered, turbulent, and coarse part—will he not shrink from the exercise of this terrible power? And if one of these intrepid men could be found, would others be found? That said, such functions cannot be exercised except in a small territory; thus, it is necessary to endow a great many citizens with this power. The English have been obliged to place overseers of the poor in every village.[16] What invariably follows from this? Poverty is identified, but its causes remain unclear: poverty is an evident fact, but its causes can only be proven by reasoning that is always contestable. Since assistance inflicts only an indirect harm to society, while its refusal directly harms the poor and even the overseer himself, the overseer's decision will not be in doubt. The laws will have declared that blameless poverty alone will be given assistance, but in practice, assistance will be given to all poverty. As for this second point, I will make some similar arguments, equally drawn from experience.

We would like work to be the price of alms. But, first, are there always public works to be done? Are they equally spread throughout the entire country, in such a manner that we never see many works to be done and few people to do them in one district, and in another, many indigents to aid and few works to be done? Because this difficulty is found in every era, mustn't it become insurmountable when—as a result of civilization's progressive development, of population growth, of the effects of the poor laws themselves—the number of indigents reaches one-sixth of the total population, as in England, or one-fourth, as in other countries?

But even supposing that works to be done are always to be found, who will take the responsibility of ascertaining their urgency, of overseeing their execution, of setting their price? This man, the overseer, independently of his qualities as a great magistrate, will thus also need to have the talents, the energy, the special knowledge of a good industrial entrepreneur. He will find in the sense of duty that which personal interest itself would probably be powerless to create: the courage to force the most inactive and vicious part of the population to productive and sustained efforts. Would it be wise to flatter ourselves about this? Is it reasonable to believe it? Appealed to by the needs of the poor, the overseer will impose made-up work, or even—like that which is almost always done in England—will give wages without requiring work. The laws must be made for men and not with an eye to an ideal perfection that does not correspond to human nature or to patterns that are only rarely seen.

Every measure that establishes legal charity on a permanent basis and that gives it an administrative form thus creates an idle and lazy class, living at the expense of the industrial and working class. This, at least, is its inevitable consequence, if not its immediate result. It reproduces all of the vices of the monastic system, but without the lofty ideas of morality and of religion that often went along with it. Such a law is a poisoned seed, planted in the bosom of legislation. As in America, circumstances can prevent the seed from developing rapidly, but they cannot destroy it, and if the present generation escapes its influence, it will devour the well-being of the generations to come.

If you closely study the condition of the populations in which similar legislation has long been in force, you will easily discover that the effects are not less unfortunate for morality than for public prosperity and that it depraves men even more than it impoverishes them.

In general, there is nothing that elevates and sustains the human mind [*esprit*] more than the idea of rights. In the idea of rights, we find something grand and virile that removes the supplicant nature from the request and places him who asks on the same level as him who bestows. But the right that the poor person has to obtain society's assistance is unique, in that rather than elevating the heart of the man who exercises it, it debases him. In countries in which legislation has never offered such a remedy, it is true that the poor person, in appealing to individual charity, recognizes his inferior state in relation to his fellow beings, but he recognizes it in secret and for a moment. From the moment the indigent is inscribed on the list of parish poor, he can certainly demand assistance, but what is the obtaining of this right, if not a formalized manifestation of the poverty, weakness, and misconduct of the one in whom that right is vested? Ordinary rights are conferred upon men because of some personal advantage acquired by them over their fellow beings. This right is bestowed because of a recognized inferiority. The first emphasizes and records that advantage; the second highlights this inferiority and legalizes it.

The greater and more secure these first types of rights are, the more they are honored; the more the other type is permanent and widespread, the more it degrades.

The poor person who demands alms in the name of the law is thereby in a still more humiliating position than the indigent who asks his fellow beings for alms out of pity and in the name of the one who sees the poor and the rich with the same eye and who subjects them to equal laws.

But that is not all: individual alms establish precious ties between the rich man and the poor one. The act of generosity itself makes the giver interested in the one whose poverty he has undertaken to relieve. The second, supported by assistance that he had no right to demand and that he perhaps did not hope to obtain, feels himself drawn by gratitude. A moral link is established between these two classes that have so many interests and passions contributing to their separation, and, though they are divided by fortune, their will brings them together. Legal charity is not like this. Alms remain, but their morality is removed. The rich man, whom the law strips of a part of his surplus without consulting him, sees in the poor man only a greedy stranger, summoned by the legislator to share his goods. From his side, the poor man feels no gratitude for a benefit that could not be denied him and that would not in any case satisfy him, for public alms, which ensure life, do not make it any more happy or comfortable than individual almsgiving does. Legal charity thus does not prevent there being a class of poor and a class of rich in society, with one looking around with fear or hatred and the other thinking about their troubles with despair and envy. Far from tending to unite into a single people these two rival nations that are called the rich and the poor and that have existed since the beginning of the world, legal charity breaks the only line that could have been established between them. It arranges each under its banner, counts them, and bringing them face-to-face, readies them for combat.

I have said that the inevitable result of legal charity is to keep the greatest number of poor in idleness and to maintain their leisure at the expense of those who work.

If idleness in the midst of wealth, the hereditary idleness earned by works or services, the idleness surrounded with public regard, accompanied by inner contentment [*le contentement d'esprit*], interested by the pleasures of the mind, moralized by the exercise of thought—if this idleness, I say, has been the mother of so many vices, what will come from a degraded idleness acquired from cowardice, earned by misconduct, that is enjoyed amid ignominy and that can only be endured to the extent that the soul of the one who suffers it becomes completely corrupted and degraded?

For what is there to hope for from a man whose position cannot be improved, because he has lost the respect of his fellows, which is the first condition of all progress; whose luck will not become worse, because having been reduced to the satisfaction on his most pressing needs, he is assured that they will always be satisfied? What action for conscience and human activity remains in a being so limited in every way, who lives without hope and without fear because he knows the future, as an animal does, because he ignores destiny's circumstances, and who is thus focused like the animal in the present and in the ignoble and fleeting pleasures that the present offers to a brutalized nature?

Read all the books written in England on pauperism. Study the investigations ordered by the British Parliament. Look at the discussions that took place in the House of Lords and in the Commons on this difficult question. One single cry will ring out to your ears: we deplore the degraded state into which the inferior classes of this great people have fallen! The number of illegitimate children has risen continuously; that of criminals has grown incessantly. The indigent population is increasing greatly; the spirit of foresight and of saving becomes more and more foreign to the poor. While enlightenment expands throughout the rest of the nation, mores become gentler, taste becomes more delicate, habits more polite—the poor remain immobile or regress; one could say that they fall back toward barbarism while in the midst of civilization's wonders, their ideas and inclinations bring them closer to savages.

Legal charity's effects on the poor man's liberty are as disastrous as its effects on his morality. This is easily demonstrable: from the moment villages are given a strict duty to assist indigents, it immediately and necessarily follows that villages owe assistance only to the poor domiciled in their territory. This is the only fair way of equalizing the public burden, which results from the law, and of making it proportionate to the means of those who must bear it. Since individual charity is almost unknown in a country in which public charity is organized, it can happen that he whose misfortunes or vices render him incapable of earning a living is sentenced, under pain of death, not to leave the place in which he was born. If he leaves, he is only going to enemy territory: individual interest within the villages, otherwise strong and much more active than the best-organized national police force, denounces his arrival, watches his every move, and, if he wants to take up residency somewhere new, refers him to the public authority, who brings back him to the place of departure. By their Poor Laws, the English have *immobilized* one-sixth of their population. They have tied them to land, just as the medieval peasants were. Villeinage *forced* the individual, *against his will*, to remain where he was born; legal charity *stops him from wanting* to move away. This is the only difference I see between the two systems. The English have gone further, and from the principle of public charity, they have drawn what I think are the most disastrous effects. The English villages are so preoccupied with the fear that an individual might fall into their charge and might obtain domicile in their midst that when a stranger whose appearance does not announce opulence settles momentarily among them or when an unexpected misfortune strikes him, the municipal authority hastens to demand a security deposit against future poverty, and if the foreigner cannot not furnish this deposit, he must leave.

Thus, legal charity has taken the freedom of movement not only from the poor of England but also from all those whom poverty menaces.

I would not know, I think, how better to complete this sad picture than by transcribing here the following passage that I find in my notes on England.

I traveled throughout Great Britain in 1833. Others were struck by the prosperity of the country: I reflected upon the hidden restlessness[17] that manifestly exercised the minds of all its inhabitants. I thought that great miseries must have been hidden under this brilliant mantle that Europe admires. This idea led me to examine with special attention pauperism, this hideous and immense tumor attached to a healthy and vigorous body.

I was then staying in the house of a large landowner in the south of England; it was when the justices of the peace were meeting to pass judgments about the claims that the poor brought against the village, or the village against the poor. My host was a justice of the peace, and I regularly accompanied him to court. In my travel notes, I find this sketch of the first hearing I attended; it summarizes in a few words and brings into relief everything I have said until now. I transcribe with painstaking precision in order to give the simple stamp of truth to the scene.

"The first individual presenting himself before the justices of the peace is an old man. His face is fresh and rosy, he is wigged and wearing an excellent black outfit. He seems to be a man of independent means. He approaches the bench and, enraged, complains about the injustice of his commune's administrators. This man is a pauper,[18] and his share of the public charity has just been unjustly diminished. The case is postponed in order for the village administrators to be heard.

"After this hearty and petulant old man appears a pregnant young woman whose clothing attests to recent poverty and whose faded features bear the imprint of her sufferings. She explains that her husband left several days ago for a sea voyage, and that because she has received neither news nor support from him since then, she is asking for public alms, but the overseer of the poor[19] hesitates to give it to her. The father-in-law of this woman is a well-off merchant. He lives in the same town in which the court holds its sessions, and it is hoped that he will want, in the absence of his son, to take responsibility for the maintenance of his daughter-in-law. The justices of the peace summon this man, but he refuses to fulfill the duties that nature imposes upon him but which the law does not demand from him. The magistrates insist; they attempt to inspire remorse or compassion in this man's selfish[20] soul. Their efforts fail, and the village is sentenced to pay the requested relief.

"After this poor, abandoned woman come five or six large and vigorous men. They are in the force of youth; their manner is firm and almost insulting. They complain about the administrators of their villages, who refuse to give them work, or in the place of work, assistance.

"The administrators reply that the village has no work to carry out at this moment; and as for free assistance, they say it is not required, because the plaintiffs could easily find employment with private individuals, if they wanted to.

"Lord X,[d] with whom I had come, said to me: 'In a small setting, you have just seen one part of the numerous abuses that the Poor Laws produce. This old man, who came forward first, probably has enough to live on, but he thinks that he has the right to demand that he be supported in comfort, and he does not blush to ask for public charity, which has, in the eyes of the people, lost its painful and humiliating character. That young woman, who seems honest and unfortunate, would certainly have been taken care of by her father-in-law if the Poor Laws did not exist, but interest silences the cry of shame within him, and he unloads on the public a debt that he alone should pay. As for the young people who presented themselves last, I know them and they live in my village: they are very dangerous citizens, and in fact, bad subjects. They quickly spend in pubs the money they

d. Lord Radnor.

earn because they know that the state will come to their assistance; thus, they see that at the first difficulty, caused by their own fault, they appeal to us.'

"The audience continues. A young woman comes before the bench; her village's overseer of the poor follows her, and a child accompanies her. She approaches without the smallest sign of hesitation; modesty does not even make her lower her gaze. The overseer accuses her of having had the baby she carries in her arms through illicit sexual intercourse.

"She agrees to this without discomfort. As she is indigent, and as the illegitimate baby, if the father remains unknown, becomes with its mother the responsibility of the village, the overseer orders her to name the father. The court puts her under oath. She names a neighborhood peasant. This man, who is present in the audience, complacently admits the accuracy of the statement, and the justices of the peace sentence him to support the child. The father and the mother retire, without this incident stirring the least emotion in the assembly, which is accustomed to these types of spectacles.

"After this young woman, another presents herself. This one comes voluntarily; she approaches the magistrates with the same insolent carelessness that the first young woman had shown. She states that she is pregnant and names the father of unborn child; this man is absent. The court postpones the matter to another day in order to have him summoned.

"Lord X says to me: 'Here are more of the disastrous effects produced by the same laws. The most direct consequence of the Poor Laws is to make the support of abandoned babies, who are the neediest of all indigents, a public expense. From this is born the desire to release the villages from supporting illegitimate children whose parents would be capable of taking care of them. From this also comes the inquiry into paternity brought about by the village and whose proof is left to the woman. For what other type of proof can one pride oneself on obtaining in such a situation? In requiring the villages to care for illegitimate children and in allowing the villages to investigate paternity in order to lighten this overwhelming burden, we have facilitated as much as we could the misconduct of lower-class women. Illegitimate pregnancies must almost always improve these women's material situation. If the father of the child is rich, the woman can hand over to him the responsibility of raising the fruit of their joint error; if he is poor, these women can confer this responsibility upon society. The assistance that is given to them from one or the other almost always surpasses the newborn's expenses. Thus, they enrich themselves by their very vices, and it often happens that the daughter who has many times been a mother makes a more advantageous marriage than the young virgin who has only her virtues to offer. The first finds a kind of dowry in her infamy.'"

I repeat that I wanted to change nothing in this passage from my journal. I have reproduced it in the same words, because it seemed to have simply and truthfully given the impressions that I wanted to share with the reader.

Since my journey to England, the poor laws have been modified. Many Englishmen flatter themselves that these changes will have a great influence on the indigents' future, on their morality, and on their number. I would like to share these hopes, but I would not know how. In this new law, today's Englishmen have again consecrated the principle acknowledged 250 years ago by Elizabeth. Like this princess, they have imposed upon society the obligation to feed the poor. This is enough. All of the abuses I have tried to describe are contained in the first principle like the largest oak tree, whose acorn can be held in the hand of a child. It needs only time to develop and to grow. To wish to establish a law which regularly, permanently, and uniformly gives assistance to indigents, without their number increasing, their laziness growing with their needs, their idleness with their vices, is to plant the acorn and to be stunned, first, when a stem appears, then leaves, later flowers, and finally fruits, which, spreading widely, will one day give forth a green forest from the depths of the earth.

I am certainly far from wanting to put on trial beneficence, which is simultaneously the most beautiful and most sacred of virtues. But I think that there is no principle so good that its consequences are only good. I believe that beneficence must be a manly and reasoned virtue, not a feeble and thoughtless inclination. I believe that it is necessary not to do the good that pleases most of those who give, but that which is truly useful for the recipient; not that which most completely relieves the miseries of some, but that which serves the well-being of the greatest number. I would know how to measure beneficence only in this manner; taken in another sense, it is still a sublime instinct, but in my view, it does not deserve the name of virtue.

I acknowledge that individual charity almost always produces useful effects. It addresses the largest miseries; it walks quietly behind misfortune and, unannounced and silently, repairs the ills that misfortune has caused. It shows up everywhere there are unfortunates to assist; it grows with sufferings. One cannot, however, count on it without recklessness, because a thousand accidents can slow or stop its workings. One does not know where it can be found, and it is not aroused by the cry of all sufferings.

I admit that by regulating aid, associations of charitable people could give greater activity and power to individual beneficence.[21] I recognize not only the utility, but also the necessity, of a public charity applied to inevitable evils such as infant frailty, the failings of old age, illness, insanity. I also admit its momentary usefulness in times of public emergency which from time to time emanate from the hands of God, to tell nations of his anger. State alms are then as instantaneous, as unforeseen, and as fleeting as the evil itself.

I even understand public charity opening schools for the children of the poor and freely supplying intelligence with the means to achieve, through work, the goods of the body.

But I am deeply convinced that any regularized, permanent, administrative system whose goal is to provide for the needs of the poor will give birth to more miseries than it is able to heal, will deprave the population it wants to aid and console, will over time reduce the rich to being but the tenant-farmers of the poor, will dry up the springs of savings, will halt the accumulation of capital, will reduce the growth of commerce, will dull human activity and industry, and will end by bringing a violent revolution in the state when the number of those who receive alms becomes as large as the number of those giving them and when the indigent, not able to draw from the impoverished rich what is necessary for their needs, find it easier to strip them suddenly of their goods than to demand assistance from them.

Let us briefly summarize everything that has preceded:

The progressive march of modern civilization gradually increases, and in a proportion that is more or less rapid, the number of those who are brought to appeal to charity.

What remedy can be brought to such evils?

Legal alms comes to mind first—legal alms in all of its forms: now free, now disguised under the form of a wage, now accidental and fleeting in certain times, now regular and permanent in others. But a deep examination quickly demonstrates that this remedy, which seems both so natural and so efficacious, is a dangerous undertaking. In whatever manner it is used, it brings but a false and momentary relief to individual sorrows, and it aggravates society's wounds.

Thus, we are left with individual charity. It knows how to produce only useful effects. Its very weakness protects it from its dangers. It relieves many miseries and gives birth to none. But faced with the progressive development of industrial classes and all of the evils that civilization mixes with the inestimable goods it produces, individual charity appears quite weak. Though sufficient in the Middle Ages, when religious fervor gave it immense energy and when its task was therefore less difficult to complete, what will it become today, when the burden it must bear is heavy and when its powers are weakened? Individual charity is a powerful agent that society must not scorn, but to which it would be imprudent to entrust itself: it is one means, but it cannot be the sole one.

What, then, is left to be done? Where should we look? How can we reduce the evils that we have the ability to see but not to heal?

Until now, I have examined the monetary solution to poverty. But is there nothing other than this type of solution? After we have dreamt of relieving the evils, would it not be useful to look to prevent them? Can we not prevent the rapid movement of the population, so that men do not leave the land and go over to industry except to the extent that industry can easily respond to their needs? Can the total national wealth continue to grow without the part that produces this wealth having to curse the prosperity they have generated? Is it impossible to establish a more permanent and regular connection between the production and the consumption of manufactured goods? Can we not foster among the working classes the accumulation of savings, which would, in times of industrial disaster, allow them to await better fortunes without dying?

The horizon opens before me here. My subject grows larger. I see a path opening, but at this moment, I cannot follow it. The present memoir, too short for that which I had to treat, already exceeds the limits that I believed necessary to set for myself. The aid measures with which one can hope to be able to combat pauperism in a preventive manner will be the focus of a second report with which I intend to pay tribute to the Academic Society of Cherbourg next year.

SECOND MEMOIR
ON PAUPERISM

(1837)

In an earlier article, I tried to show that today's public and private charities are powerless to cure the miseries of the poor classes. It remains for me to search for the means that might be used to prevent these miseries from arising.

Such a subject is almost without natural limits, and I feel the need to place boundaries on myself that are not indicated by the subject.

Among those whose situation places them at the threshold of need and to which the subject of this article refers, it is appropriate to establish two broad categories: on one side are found the poor belonging to the agricultural classes; on the other side, the poor who are a part of the industrial classes. These two aspects of my subject must be taken separately and examined in detail at least as much as the narrow limits of the present work will allow.

I will only touch lightly on what pertains to the agricultural classes, since the great menaces of the future do not come from there.

In France, substitutions[1] have been abolished, and equality of shares has penetrated mores at the same time that it was established in laws. Thus, it is certain that in France, property ownership will never be concentrated in a few hands, as is still seen in parts of Europe.

Now the same division of land that could harm—at least temporarily—agricultural progress by preventing the concentration of capital in the hands of property owners who wanted to innovate produces this immense good: it forestalls the development of pauperism in the agricultural classes. When, as was the case in England, the peasant did not possess any part of the land, the masters' caprices or greed could suddenly inflict terrible miseries upon the peasant. This is easily understood. The same number of men is not necessary for all types of farming, nor called for by every method of farming.

When, for example, you convert wheat fields into pasture, one shepherd could easily replace a hundred cultivators. When you make one large farm out of twenty smaller ones, a hundred men would suffice to cultivate the same fields that used to call for four hundred hands. From the technical point of view, there has perhaps been progress in the conversion of wheat fields to grasslands and of small farms into large holdings, but the peasant at whose expense such experiments are conducted cannot fail to suffer from them. I have heard from a wealthy Scottish landowner that a change in the manner of managing and cultivating his lands forced three thousand peasants to leave their homes and go to seek their fortunes elsewhere. The agricultural population of that burgh of Scotland thus found itself suddenly exposed to the same miseries that constantly strike the industrial populations when new machines are discovered.

Such events give rise to pauperism among the agricultural classes, as well as to its disproportionate growth among the industrial classes. Men who are thus violently ripped from the cultivation of the earth seek refuge in workshops and factories.

Hence, the industrial class grows not only in a natural and haphazard manner according to industrial needs but also suddenly and by an artificial process following the miseries of the agricultural class. This latter process quickly produces a surplus and destroys the balance that should always exist between consumption and production.

The concentration of landed property into a small number of hands has not only accidentally resulted in bringing misery to a portion of the agricultural class but also has given a large number of farmers ideas and habits that will necessarily make them miserable in the long run.

What do we see before our own eyes every day? Which members of the inferior classes most freely succumb to every excess of intemperance and love to live as if each day has no tomorrow? Which ones show the greatest lack of foresight in everything? Who contracts those premature and imprudent marriages that seem to have no other object than to multiply the number of the earth's unhappy inhabitants?

The response is simple. They are the proletarians, those who have no other property under the sun than their own labor. As these same men come to possess any portion of land, however small, do you not notice that their ideas modify and that their habits change? Is it not apparent that with landed property comes thought of the future? From the moment they feel they have something precious to lose, they become prudent. As soon as they believe themselves to be the means of removing themselves and their children from poverty's ravages, they take energetic measures to escape poverty, and by momentary privations, they seek to assure themselves of a lasting well-being. These people are not yet wealthy, but they already have those qualities that give birth to wealth. Franklin was in the habit of saying that with order, activity, and economy, the road to fortune was as easy as the road to the market.[2] He was right.

Thus, it is not poverty that makes the farmer imprudent and reckless, because with a very small field, he could still be very poor. It is the complete absence of all property; it is the absolute subjection to chance.

I add that among the means of giving men the feeling of order, activity and economy, I have never known a more powerful one than facilitating their access to landed property.

Again, I will cite the example of the English. Taken as a whole, the peasants in England are perhaps more enlightened[3] and they do not appear to be less industrious than the ones here. Why do they generally live in this beast-like indifference for tomorrow, of which we have not even the idea? From whence does a cold people get this reckless taste for imprudence? Simple: in England, the laws and habits have combined so that no portion of land ever falls into the possession of the poor person. Neither his well-being nor even his existence ever depends on himself, but instead on the will of the wealthy people against whom he can do nothing and who can give or refuse him work as they please. Not having any direct and permanent influence over his own future, he ceases to concern himself with it and willingly forgets that it exists.

Thus, the most efficacious means of preventing pauperism among the agricultural classes is most certainly the division of land. We have this division in France; thus, one should not fear that large and permanent wretchedness would ever be established among them. But the comfort of these classes could be greatly expanded and bad individuals among them could be made rarer and less cruel. The duty of government and of all good people is to work for this.

It is beyond my present subject to search for the means [of doing these things].

If the agricultural class in France is not as exposed to inevitable reverses as elsewhere, the industrial class is hardly less so. The remedy that we have successfully applied to the miseries of the farmer has not been—and it is unlikely ever to be—applied to the woes of the industrial worker.

Unlike with landed property, we have still not discovered a way of dividing industrial property so that it is not made unproductive; industry has preserved the aristocratic form in modern nations, although everywhere, we see the institutions and mores born of aristocracy fading away.

Until now, experience has shown that in order to engage in most commercial enterprises with any hope of success, large capital concentrated in a small number of hands is necessary. Thus, we find a few individuals who possess great wealth and who put to work on their behalf a multitude of workers who possess nothing themselves. Such is the spectacle that French industry presents nowadays. It is exactly what happened here in the Middle Ages and what we see still happening to agricultural industry over much of Europe.

The results are similar. Today's worker, like the farmer of the Middle Ages, having no property that belongs to him and seeing no way of securing his future tranquility and of gradually raising himself up to wealth by his own efforts, becomes indifferent to everything that is not present enjoyment. His indifference delivers him, defenseless, to every chance of misery. But this great and essential difference exists between the agricultural proletariat and the industrial proletariat: the latter, regardless of the habitual miseries to which his lack of foresight might deliver him, is still incessantly exposed to accidental evils that he cannot foresee and which do not menace the former. And these chances are infinitely larger in actual industry than in agriculture, because as we will explain below, industry is subject to sudden crises that agriculture has never known.

These unforeseeable evils lead to commercial crises. Commercial crises are permanently attributable to two causes:

- When the number of workers increases without production figures varying, salaries diminish, and there is a crisis.

- When the number of workers remains the same, but production figures fall, many workers become superfluous, and there is a crisis.

We have seen that France is much less exposed than other industrial nations to the first type of crisis, because our agricultural class is never suddenly and violently forced into industry.

France is also much less exposed than other manufacturing peoples to the second type of crisis, because she depends less on foreign countries. Let me explain.

When one nation's industry depends on the whims or the needs of foreign nations, of faraway and almost unknown nations, it is easy to see that as these whims or needs happen to change as a result of causes that could not be foreseen, an industrial revolution is always to be feared. By contrast, when the sole or principal consumer of a country's products is found within that same country, its needs and its tastes would not be able to vary in such a sudden and unforeseen manner that the producer would not be able to discover well in advance the impending change and, the change itself only taking effect gradually, there is discomfort in commerce, but there is rarely a crisis.

The world is obviously headed toward that point at which all nations will be equally civilized, or in other terms, similar enough to each other to be able to produce domestically the majority of products they need and desire. Commercial crises will thus become rarer and less severe. But we are still far from this time; today, there are still sufficient inequalities of enlightenment, power, and industry among peoples, so that some of them can take care of producing the objects that a large number of the others need. These peoples, entrepreneurs in human industry, easily amass immense riches, but they are incessantly threatened by terrible dangers.

Such is England's position. France's commercial situation is both less brilliant and more secure. France only exports abroad the . . .[4] of her products; the rest are sold domestically. Our aggregate consumption continually rises, but our new consumers are generally French.

In France, therefore, commercial crises can be neither as frequent nor as widespread nor as cruel as they are in England. But we would not know what to do if there were ever a crisis, because we lack the means to balance—in a permanent and exact manner, even within the kingdom itself—the number of workers and the amount of work, consumption and production.

One can thus foresee that the industrial classes, regardless of the general and permanent causes of poverty that affect them, will frequently be subjected to crises. It is therefore quite necessary to be able to protect them both from the evils that they bring upon themselves and from those evils against which they can do nothing. The whole question is how to know which preventive means they should use in order to mitigate the effects of those evils.

In my opinion, the crux of the problem to be solved is this:

To find a means of giving the worker the small farmer's spirit and habits of property ownership.

Two principal means of doing this present themselves: the first, which initially seems the most efficacious, would consist in giving the worker an interest in the factory. This would produce effects in the industrial class similar to the division of landed property among the agricultural class.

It would be beyond the limits of this work to examine all of the plans that have successively been proposed in order to achieve this result.

I will therefore content myself with briefly saying that these plans have always encountered two obstacles to their success: on the one hand, industrial capitalist entrepreneurs [*les capitalistes entrepreneurs d'industrie*] have almost all shown themselves little inclined to give their workers a proportionate amount of profits or to contribute to the company small sums which could be shared by the workers. I think that from their own perspective [*dans leur intérêt*], they have made a grave mistake in not doing this, but it would be neither just nor useful to require it of them. On the other hand, when workers have wanted to do without capitalists,[5] to form their own associations, to raise money and to manage their work with the help of a trade union, they have not been able to succeed. Disorder has not been long in entering into the association, [or] its agents have been unfaithful, [or] its capital insufficient or unstable, [or] its credit virtually nonexistent, [or] its commercial relations very restricted. Ruinous competition would soon force the association to dissolve itself. Such attempts have often been repeated before our very eyes—particularly in the past seven years—but always in vain.

Nevertheless, I am led to believe that a time is approaching when a large number of industries might be run in this manner. As our workers gain broader knowledge and as the art of associating together [*s'associer*] for honest and peaceful goals makes progress among us, when politics does not meddle in industrial associations and when government, reassured about their goals, does not refuse them its benevolence and its support, we will see them multiply and prosper. In democratic ages like ours, I think that associations of all sorts must gradually come to take the place of the commanding action of a few powerful individuals.

It thus seems to me that the idea of workers' industrial associations is bound to be a fertile one, but I do not think it is ripe. Therefore, it is presently necessary to seek remedies elsewhere.

Since one cannot give workers an interest in the ownership of the factory, one can at least help them in the creation of their independent property, with the aid of their salaries drawn from the factory.

Encouraging the saving of salaries and offering workers an easy and reliable method to build these savings and to make them generate returns—such are thus the only means society can nowadays use in its goal of fighting the negative effects of the concentration of movable property in the same hands and the only means to give the industrial class the spirit and habits of property that a large portion of the agricultural class possesses.

The entire question thus boils down to seeking means that would permit the poor to build their savings and render them productive.

The first of these means, and the only one that has been used in France up to now, is the establishment of savings banks.

So I will speak at some length about savings banks. French savings banks differ slightly among themselves in administrative detail, but they can ultimately all be thought of as establishments through which poor people place their savings in the hands of the State, which is tasked with investing them profitably and earning 4 percent interest on them.

It is more or less the same in England, except the interest paid by the State is a little lower than here.

Doesn't such a remedy present grave dangers?

First, I note that in France, the State, which gives poor people 4 percent of their money, could easily borrow at 2.5 or 3 percent. Thus, it is at least 1 percent that the state needlessly and for special reasons pays to its creditors. The resulting sum must be considered as the product of a genuine poor tax that the government levies on all taxpayers in order to help the neediest of them.

Would the State want to bear this burden for a long time? Could it? This seems very doubtful.

In just a few years, the total in our savings banks has risen to more than one hundred million. Right now, it is four hundred million in England.[6] In Scotland, which has but 2,300,000 inhabitants, poor people's savings total almost four hundred million.

If France's poor classes bring four or five hundred million into the Public Treasury, in a period in which paying 4 percent interest is possible and even likely, would the Treasury be in a position to accept that money? Even if the interest were reduced, which would already be a great misfortune, wouldn't such an amount often be much more embarrassing than useful?

The current setup of our savings banks is thus troublesome for the Treasury. Does their creation offer desirable protections to the nation and to the poor themselves? I do not think so.

What employment could the State find for these sums that are being deposited in its hands from all corners of France?

Will it employ them to provide for the Treasury's daily needs? But the Treasury's needs are limited, and the growth of savings banks is not. A moment therefore comes when the State, receiving more than it is able to spend, is forced to let immense amounts of unproductive capital accumulate in its hands. This is what we have recently seen. When the recent law about savings banks was presented (February 1837), the Treasury had sixty-four million in ready cash in the bank, of which it paid 4 percent to owners and which yields the Treasury nothing, and which is entirely removed from circulation, always an unfortunate measure.

Because of this, one of the speakers who took part in the discussion of the recent law said that it was necessary to create expenditures in order to consume capital—an idea that has been developed by other speakers who have spoken of large public works that would be undertaken with the workers' savings. Because these works would not or could not be productive for the State, all of this ultimately boils down to burdening, each year, the mass of taxpayers with the interest on the sums that the poor have deposited in the Public Treasury. This would obviously be a poor tax, under another name.

If the State does not use the money in the savings banks to provide for the Treasury's daily needs, it is necessary to position the money so that it yields the Treasury interest. Now, it is easy to see that there is only one appropriate investment, the purchase of bonds. The State is the holder of the savings banks' money only under the condition of returning it at the depositors' first demand; thus, it cannot itself invest depositors' money except under the same condition—that is, with the ability to liquidate on demand, in order to pay its creditor. Now, only bonds which are negotiable on the spot are able to do that on a large scale. Thus, the State, whether represented by the Treasury or by the Deposits and Consignments Fund, is able to place the funds of the poor only in bonds. This has many serious inconveniences, but particularly this one: when the poor deposit money, bonds are purchased continually and at high prices, precisely because many are being purchased at once; when there is a panic or serious misfortune and the poor ask for their money, bonds have to be sold in order to pay them, and they are always sold at low prices, for the reason that many are sold at once. The State is thus placed in this deplorable position, where it always has to buy high and sell low, which means losing money.

This account is accurate and I think that no one would currently consider disputing it.

Hence, depositing poor people's money in the hands of the State is or could easily become very onerous to the State, and, what is worse, it could impose upon the State charges whose extent is impossible to anticipate in advance.

That is not all. Is this in conformity with the country's general interest and safety? From the economic point of view, I think it is harmful to incessantly bring to the center all the small pools of capital available in the provinces, for they might be used to enrich localities. I know that some of this capital returns to the localities in the form of government officials' salaries and public works . . .[7] But this return of money from the center to the extremities occurs slowly and unequally; the biggest sums are often spread out across provinces that have given the least to the Treasury and that are, being poorer and more backward, in the greatest need of having roads built, canals dug, and so on. Moreover, it is always just a part of the savings of the poor that returns to them in the form of salaries or social improvements. The bulk, especially after the new law, will get lost in the public funds and remain in commercial or bondholders' hands in Paris.

If I consider the present system from a purely political point of view, its dangers strike me even more.

Personally, I cannot believe that it would be wise to place the entire fortune of a large kingdom's poor classes in the same hands, and so to speak, in a single place, in such a way that an event—surely improbable, but possible—could in one stroke ruin their last and only resources and bring to despair entire populations who, no longer having anything to lose, would more readily descend upon the possessions of others.

In the last one hundred years, the State has declared bankruptcy more than once: the Old Regime did it, the Convention did it. During the past fifty years, France's government has been radically changed seven times, and it has been reorganized many other times. In this same period, the French have had twenty-five years of terrible war and two almost complete invasions of their territory. It is painful to recall these facts, but prudence demands that we not forget them. In a transitional age such as ours, in an age that has been forcefully brought to long agitations by its timing and nature, in such an age, is it wise to deliver into the hands of government, whatever be its form and its present representative, the entire fortune[8] of such a large number of men? I cannot believe it is, and I need to have proven to me that such a thing is necessary before I submit to it.

Moreover, what must be feared is not only that the government seizes the capital loaned by the poor but also that the lenders, by their own imprudence, make it impossible for their creditor to return the capital and force it to go bankrupt.[9]

What is the goal of savings banks? To permit the poor person to gradually accumulate capital during prosperous years that they can use in times of misfortune. It is thus in the very essence of savings banks that repayment be always payable and in small sums—that is, in cash.

In a moment of national crisis, in a time of revolution, when real or imaginary fears about the Public Treasury's solvency could suddenly strike the people's minds, it would thus be possible that within a few days, the State could be instructed to pay out, *in cash*, many hundreds of millions of francs. This is something, however, that it would not be able to do. And yet, who would dare calculate the effect that the announcement of such an event[10] would have upon all of the indigent classes in a large kingdom like France?

With the commendable intention of allaying the ill-founded fears to which the latest law about savings banks has given birth in the minds of the Parisian working class, M. Charles Dupin[11] has recently tried to establish that in France, savings bank deposits cannot exceed certain fixed limits, the ceiling of which he sets at about 250 million, already a considerable sum, but one that the State could nevertheless surely manage.

In order to head off the argument that would be inevitably drawn from the example of England and above all from the example of Scotland, where with a population of a little more than two million inhabitants, savings banks—founded for only thirty-six years [*sic*]—have already received deposits amounting to four hundred million francs, M. Charles Dupin remarks that in England, it is only by depositing funds in savings banks that the lower classes, unable to own land, are able to succeed in using their savings.

The facts are true, but the conclusion drawn from them is extremely exaggerated. Whether saving is done with the goal of buying land or bonds is of little importance. The operative fact[12] is saving, and not the final objective of the savings.

I will go even further and say that, if real and absolute trust in the solvency of savings banks were to be established among France's agricultural classes, one would see—all other things being equal—infinitely more money flooding into accounts than is put into them in England. The reason for this is simple: among us, the peasant is frugal, but he economizes with the sole goal of buying land. His money thus has but one use, or no use. Here in

France, then, there is much more small capital available for the savings bank than there is in other places, and there are many more who would take this route, were it not for an instinctive fear that experience would surely diminish but that now keeps capital in the hands of those who possess it.

It is evident that as enlightenment grows and as the habit of seeking to use one's daily savings expands among France's poor classes, the small landed proprietor will no longer be piling up pennies in some quarter of his house—the total of which is supposed to allow him to expand his lands—and will thus no longer be leaving a small amount of capital unproductive and exposed to thousands of accidents over a long sequence of years. This small farmer, I say, will undoubtedly bring his savings to the local savings bank with the idea of one day withdrawing those savings from it in order to make the land acquisition that he desires. Savings banks are precisely the sole appropriate investments for those types of people who, wanting only to buy small pieces of land in their immediate neighborhood, need always to have available capital in order to be always in position to instantly seize the rare opportunities that present themselves.

The French peasant's taste for land thus does not prevent or does not strongly prevent the growth of deposits made in the savings bank. In reality, these deposits are limited only by the poor man's ability to save and by the greater or lesser enlightenment[13] that makes him see more or less clearly that his interest lies in not leaving his savings unproductive and exposed.

This is what needs to be understood well, because peoples—like individuals—gain nothing by hiding the truth. On the contrary, both need to consider the truth directly in order to see if one might by chance find a remedy amid the bad things.

What follows from all of this?

Put simply, I am far from saying that the savings banks, with the constitution we have given them, offer a *present* danger: they pose none. I even believe that if we could find a means of making the possibility of future danger disappear, it would still be necessary to create savings banks. The physical and moral evils that cause shortsightedness and pauperism are real and immense; the evils that the remedy would bring in the long run are distant and might not ever arrive. This consideration is enough to determine my mind.[14]

All I wish to say is that it would be imprudent to believe we have found in savings banks—as we see them today—a certain remedy against future evils and that we should guard against seeing their establishment as a kind of universal panacea. Rather than being lulled to sleep by this false security, today's economists and statesmen should try on the one hand to improve savings banks' composition and on the other to create additional resources through which the poor could save.

Savings banks are an excellent means of instilling in the poor the idea of saving and of earning interest on their savings. But these banks cannot become the only safe place for the poor to deposit their savings.

Let us briefly examine these two topics.

I pretend neither to research nor, above all, to show all of the improvements that could be introduced into the system of savings banks. That would exceed the limits of this article. I only want to show the general principle that I feel should be adopted and one of the easiest applications of this principle.

Rather than trying to draw the greatest amount of savings bank income into the Treasury and into public funds, the government should exercise all its power in giving, under its guarantee, a use to these small investments that is local and that least exposes the state to a universal and sudden bank run.[15] This is the principle.

As for its application, this is what I have to say:

In every village in France, there are pawnshops that are called *monts-de-piété*.[16] These *monts-de-piété* are highly usurious establishments because they generally lend at 12 percent without any risk. It is true that the money they accumulate in this manner is used to endow almshouses,[17] so that these *monts-de-piété* can be considered as establishments which ruin the poor man, so as to prepare for him a refuge in his poverty.

This simple presentation speaks for itself. It is evident that, in the interest of the indigent classes and in the interest of order and of public morality, we should hasten to find other sources for almshouse revenues.

From the moment when the link that unites the *monts-de-piété* and the almshouses[18] is broken, nothing is more natural than to unite the *monts-de-piété* and the savings banks and to make these two things one and the same enterprise.[19]

Under this system, the administrators[20] would receive people's savings with one hand and return those savings to them with the other. Poor people who have money to lend would deposit it in the hands of the administrators, and they, in return for collateral, would return that money to those poor who might need to borrow it. The administrators would be only an intermediary between these two groups. In reality, it would be the thrifty poor or those momentarily favored by fortune who would lend their savings at interest to the wasteful or unfortunate poor.

There is nothing simultaneously simpler, more practical, and more moral than such a system: using poor people's savings in this manner would not run any risks for the state or for the poor themselves, because there is nothing more certain in the world than a collateralized loan.

Since the interest on the borrowed money would thus not be used except to pay the interest on the savings deposited by the poor person, two very useful results could be obtained simultaneously: it would no longer be necessary to demand usurious interest from the poor person who borrows at interest, and a higher interest rate could be given to the poor person who deposits his savings. The first could easily be reduced to 7 percent, and the other raised to 5 percent, which would be a double benefit.

It is true that we might find moments of general poverty in which savings bank depositors would come to reclaim their money, while the numbers of borrowers from the *monts-de-piété* would increase unduly. The administrators would thus receive less from the former and would be obliged to supply more to the latter.

It is easy to see that the danger posed by this is neither noticeable nor genuine.

No establishment enjoys more credit than a pawnshop. Those who lend it money run no risk because they have the collateral itself as the guarantee of their loan. It is for this reason that the *monts-de-piété* have always found a way to borrow cheaply even when the State or private individuals were without credit. Thus, if the administrators of whom I speak would find themselves temporarily without the savings of some poor people, they would borrow in order to cope with the collateralized loans that other poor people would be giving to them, and they would still make a profit, because they would borrow at 5 percent and lend at 7 percent.

Besides, I do not claim to be the inventor of the system that I am explaining here. The merging of the *mont-de-piété* and the savings bank took place . . .[21] years ago in one of our most important cities, in terms of philanthropic and popular institutions: the city of Metz.[22] By dint of this union, the administrators of the savings bank could pay depositors who have less than . . .[23] francs 5 percent instead of 4 percent, and the administrators of the *mont-de-piété* (who are the same people) have been able to lower the interest on securitized loans to 7 percent, while in Paris, one still only manages 12 percent. Moreover, the administrative fees of these two establishments have been cut in half since they have been brought together as one. Finally, and to complete the picture, it is necessary to add that Metz's savings bank as well as the *mont-de-piété* have come through the Revolution of 1830 and the financial crisis that followed without experiencing any significant disturbance.

So the ideas that I am explaining have experience as well as reason on their side. Why has the government, which has recently showed a genuine solicitude for the material interests of the indigent classes, not tried to take advantage of this useful experience? Why is it that, far from bringing about the union of savings banks and *monts-de-piété*, it daily resists the demands of those who appeal to it for this purpose? I can understand this only with difficulty. If one ever manages truly to draw all of the savings of the poor into the hands of the State, the ruin of the poor and of the State itself would not fail to happen. Would the government believe its safety involved linking the existence of the working classes to its own existence in such a way that one could not be destroyed without ruining them both? I then cannot believe in such a dangerous enterprise. For me, I avow that in the combination I indicated, I see the most powerful means that one could use to reap savings banks' benefits while eliminating a part of their dangers. I say "a part" because it is clear that the proposed remedy would, over a period of time, become insufficient.

If this investment has been restricted in a way that savings have not, so that savings banks' administrators are able to use the savings of the poor only in making collateralized loans, a day would certainly arrive when one would be obliged to turn away a part of the new depositors. This would be a great evil, because it would cause a continual doubt in the minds of the poor about investing savings and, consequently, a strong temptation not to save.

So I would not want the State to decisively end its savings banks for the poor. I would allow the legislation that we presently have to remain; but I would authorize the savings banks to deposit their funds in the Public Treasury only when the *monts-de-piété* could not put them to use. In this way, we would have all of the institution's advantages and we would have avoided the greatest part of its dangers.

But this is still not enough. As long as the poor person does not want to deposit his money except with the condition of being able to withdraw it upon demand, and as long as there are not certain and easy means of putting that money elsewhere, we will not obtain results that are simultaneously great and sure.

LETTER ON PAUPERISM
IN NORMANDY

[We must avoid] . . . encouraging vice and a lack of foresight in wishing to satisfy needs.[1]

4. In cases—happily rare among us—in which an inevitable poverty awaits a worthy man, the aid must always be at least the same as the going rate for work.

Once these general principles are conceded, the consequences that follow from them are not difficult to find.[2]

In towns, I think it would be necessary to form voluntary associations to which the name "Township association [*associations communales*] for the extinction of vagabondage and begging" would be given. These associations would have no political character; their goal being to stop an evil that strikes equally all parties and to which the men of all parties are equally invited. They would not be hostile to the government, but they would exist separately from it.

So that the circle of action would not be too wide, each association would not unite more than two or three townships. It would even be desirable that an association pertained only to a single township.

The association would be composed of everyone who would want to dedicate an annual sum—*of whatever amount*—for the relief of the township's poor.

All of the subscribers would meet once annually and name from among their ranks a commission of three, five, or seven members (according to the size of the township) for the distribution of the aid in the manner I have already indicated. All of the subscribers, whatever the amount of their contribution, would be eligible to be chosen as members of the administrative commission. Before finishing their term each year, the members of the commission would report to the contributors how the funds had been used; their operations would be monitored by their successors.

If the members of the association fell into need during the course of the year, they would have the right to aid before all others.

At a fixed period each year, one member of each commission would present himself at Cherbourg. There, each commission would communicate what had been done during the year, and from those documents, a general report would be composed and published, along with the names of the contributors.

It is easy to show, in very few words, what the advantages of such a system would be.

First, one would not have to fear that such associations would increase the number of poor people, because no one would be able to count on the members' aid in advance and because the members would always be free to give or to refuse according to their own wishes.

Neither would one risk making charity an insupportable burden, because no one would be obliged to remain in the association.

From the other side, the association members and the townships would draw an obvious advantage from such a system.

The person who gives nothing today because, considered in isolation, the weak offering that his fortune allows him to make is of no use, would willingly give to the association because his money, coming to be added to the group funds, would thus contribute efficiently to relieving the miseries of his neighbors. Once the association was well established, even the poor themselves would be able to place summer savings into the association's hands in order to be entitled to its benefits in the winter.[3] The poor in the countryside would do what the urban worker does when he places his small savings in a savings bank.[4] For his part, the wealthy farmer would need to give less, because the charity given by the association would be stronger and more productive than individual charity. There would be both fewer alms and fewer poor people.

Because the collective funds would be used systematically and in accordance with a fixed plan, a very small contribution would be enough to relieve a great deal of poverty. What would happen to charity is what happens daily in the industries in which many individuals of small means associate together and achieve very great undertakings by each depositing only very small sums.

Hence, in those townships in which an association would exist, we would first see the disappearance of the extreme poverty that threatens the property of the well-off even more than it threatens to the existence of the indigent. For the wealthy must understand that providence has placed them in *solidarity* with the poor and that no misfortunes in this world are entirely isolated. Thus, there would be less theft, pilfering, and disorder throughout the township, because there would be less urgent poverty needing relief.

Because the association would be able to follow a fixed course and would be free to refuse gifts, it would not allow the *squandering* of its benefits as individual charity does. And if it created work for the poor, this would always be to the township's benefit.

Townships would draw an additional advantage from the associative system I am proposing: because it would be established that the association bestows its gifts only under the condition that the recipient would not beg, we would see the disappearance of those demeaning habits that take away poverty's respectable face, that deprave childhood and most often follow a generation of indigents with a generation of thieves.[5] If the poor person scorns the association's charity in favor of shameful and uncertain resources of begging, no one would be obliged in conscience to supply that person's needs, and if he were to persist in continuing his vicious ways, the harsh laws against begging would be mercilessly applied to him.

That is not all: once an association were to be established in a township, the Township [sic] would be able to expel nonresident indigents from its midst. For, in taking care of its poor, it should insist that the other townships do the same. The inhabitants of a township in which this type of association existed would thus be logically and legally well founded in refusing all aid to nonresident indigents, and the mayor, using rigorously the power given by the law, would rightfully be able to make them vacate the land.

If the system of which I am speaking were to become widespread in a district, the superior authority would in turn take the same step, and the courts would not hesitate to condemn the vagrants who, defying reason and the law, would continue to want to find their fortune among us. But the vagrants would not even have the idea of coming here. In a township near Paris (Mareuil) a certain number of owners associated together (although for less general purposes). Not only did they eradicate begging in the township, but from that time on, there has been no talk of nonresident beggars. The latter know that they have no hope of any alms, and they do not come. From that time on, this same township has not suffered from any pilfering.

M. de Windé [?][6] has written some very good things about begging. You should read them. Édouard[7] must have them sent to you.

PAUPERISM IN AMERICA

(1833)

(Appendix 3 of the *Penitentiary Report*)

The Americans have borrowed most of their institutions related to the poor from the English.

In America, as in England, every man in need has an explicit claim[1] against the state. Charity has become a political institution.

Assistance is given to the poor in two ways: in each city, as well as in most counties, are found establishments carrying the name of *almshouses*, houses of charity, or *poorhouses*, houses of the poor. These establishments can be considered both as places of asylum and as prisons. At public expense, the neediest poor are taken in and supported there. The vagabonds that the justices of the peace send there are held and made to work there. Thus, the poorhouses simultaneously contain indigents who are not *able* to earn their living through honest work and those who do not *want* to.[2]

Independently of the assistance given in the charity houses, the administration charged with oversight of the poor has brought many more to live there.

Each year, the townships [*communes*][3] tax themselves in order to support these costs of public charity, and commissioners are appointed to watch over the usage of the funds so collected.

In providing for the needs of the poor, a generally acknowledged principle is that the State merely advances monies, which the work of the poor must reimburse. But we have seen that in America, just as in England, it was almost impossible to achieve a rigorous application of this principle in practice. Many of the poor are incapable of any work; it is this very incapacity that puts them in the State's care. Almost all of the genuine poor have contracted habits of laziness that are difficult to change. Moreover, the poor person who is shut up in a charitable home considers himself unhappy but not guilty; he questions society's right to force him into a pointless job and to keep him there against his will. For its part, the administration feels defenseless on this point: the management [*régime*] of a charitable home cannot be that of a prison, and even though the man who lives there is no longer free, one cannot treat him like a criminal.

From this are born extreme difficulties that can be considered as inherent in the system of English legislation concerning the poor, difficulties whose number have been diminished by more or less perfect administrative processes, but whose complete disappearance cannot be hoped for.

Thus, in Maryland,[4] it is established that in entering the charity home, the poor person is obliged to live there until the payment of all of the costs caused by his presence. Such is the principle laid down: but it is easy to see that its application in all cases would be very onerous to the public treasury one wants to protect. The majority of the poor are incapable of earning, through work, the money required of them; sentencing them to remain in the house of charity until they have indemnified the State would generally sentence them to perpetual detention, equally harmful for the public and for them. In declaring the law, it was therefore necessary to permit the administrators of the poor to violate it all the time in the ordinary exercise of their duties and to vest these magistrates with unlimited discretionary power. I would add that the administration, whatever care has been taken by the legislature that empowered it, remains powerless to detain against their will those indigents who want to regain their liberty. This is because, we will repeat, a poor house is not and cannot be a prison.

While the principles of Maryland's legislation for the poor have undoubtedly produced a significant reduction in the state's expenditures budget, this is perhaps not because they have increased returns on goods produced by the poor, but because they have made public charity undesirable to the poor and have thus stopped them from turning to it except in the most extreme need.

Incidentally, is a regular system of public charity harmful or useful? This is an immense question, one we are not in the position to discuss in detail or to resolve.

In this matter, poverty that is born from a physical and substantive incapacity must be carefully distinguished from poverty which arises from other causes. The State can relieve the first type without causing great harm to society. Certainly, no one would ever expose themselves to losing a limb in order to be fed at public expense. But we are persuaded that every law which comes, in a predictable and certain manner, to the assistance of the miseries of the poor will almost certainly result in continually augmenting their number. Moreover, such a law will always deprave the population that it is designed to assist. We already know what enormous sums England's poor tax has raised.[5] Should the existing state of things endure another half century, one will justly be able to say that in that country, the workers enjoy the land and the proprietors are their tenant farmers. There are few indigents in America, but that fact seems due to reasons far from the matters with which we are occupied, and it is possible that this is not due to law, but on the contrary, in spite of the law. In the United States, we noticed that legislation about pauperism was a source of all types of administrative abuses, of very great expenditures, and of innumerable difficulties of execution. It seemed to us that the lowest classes of the American people indulged in disorderly habits and acted with a lack of foresight that was primarily due to the certainty of being assisted in need. The Irishmen of large cities spend the summer in abundance and the winter in poor houses. Public charity has lost its character of shame for them, because thousands of men turn to it daily. Elsewhere in Europe, we have observed that when society's superior classes undertake to relieve the miseries of the poor, they almost always exceed the goal that they want to reach, because their imagination makes them exaggerate the sufferings that cause the poor hardships that they have never themselves endured. It is thus in America: the charitable houses we had the opportunity to visit generally provided the poor person with a refuge that was not merely healthy but also agreeable; there, he finds well-being and enjoyments that honest labor in the outside world probably would not provide him.

To these preliminary reflections, we add the statistical table of the number of poor people in the state of New York in 1830 and of the totals that have been spent for their maintenance: this table will be used to give a very precise idea of pauperism in America. As we know, the state of New York is the largest in the union, and nothing suggests that the number of indigents must be less there than elsewhere.

In 1830, the state of New York was divided into fifty-five administrative districts, called *counties* [*comtés*]; in each of these counties reside three or five administrators called *superintendents of the poor*. These magistrates see to it that assistance is provided to indigents; they have had built and maintain the county's charitable houses, and they direct their governance. Each year, the necessary funds are levied, following the vote of an elected body called *the board of supervisors*,[6] which represents the county. According to the letter of the law, the superintendents of the poor must provide an annual account of their administration to the state central government. It is an extract of these different annual reports that we are going to present.

Only forty-four districts, containing one million six hundred fifty-three thousand eight hundred forty-five inhabitants, sent their reports in 1830.[a]

It follows from these documents that in the forty-four counties, fifteen thousand five hundred and six poor people were assisted; that means one poor person for every one hundred and seven inhabitants.[b] Among the fifteen thousand five hundred and six poor people are two thousand three hundred and seventy-six individuals not resident in the state of New York; thus, the remainder is one poor person for every one hundred and twenty-six inhabitants of the state of New York.

The work of these fifteen thousand five hundred and six individuals has saved the state an outlay that could be evaluated in 1830 at 10,674 dollars.

In the course of the year, then, each poor person needs to earn only 70 cents or 3 francs 71 centimes.

Making a deduction for what is produced by their labor, the maintenance of these fifteen thousand five hundred and six individuals has cost the state at least 216,535 dollars;[c] this would give an annual expenditure of 14 dollars or 74 francs for each poor person.

---

a. The secretary of the state, in his report to the legislative body, signals this important omission on the part of the local administrations of eleven counties. But he establishes the fact without accompanying it with any observations. In America, the central authority seems merely to be tolerated and conceals itself as much as possible. In the state of New York, the only one in which a shadow of centralization is found, there are already very loud complaints about the power accorded to the government.

b. Evaluations whose foundations are, it is true, rather uncertain, place the number of poor in France at around one out of sixteen inhabitants.

c. We say *at least* because, in effect, many counties did not note administrative costs—which are, however, very considerable—in their reports.

The administrative and court costs alone have risen to 27,981 dollars or 158,299 francs.

Thus, in 1830, New York State's tax pertaining to the support of the poor came to 13 cents or 69 centimes per inhabitant.

Independently of these annual expenditures, the grounds and buildings that the state dedicates to the feeding and housing of the poor create a considerable capital.

Recently, the State of New York has begun a system of agricultural colonies[7] to support the poor.[d] In the forty-four counties of which we have spoken, three thousand eight hundred and seventy-eight acres of good land have been allocated for this use. These lands generally belonged to the state and have been acquired by it at a very low price. In dedicating them to the indigent, the state has greatly diminished the burden on the public treasury, and the poor are busied with works that are entirely their own. Here is another of the greatest advantages that the United States has over England.

In 1830, the capital thus engaged by the State of New York was evaluated at 757,257 dollars or 4,013,409 francs.

---

d. When we say that the system of agricultural colonies has been implemented for the support of the poor, we do not mean to say that the example of Holland has been imitated. In both countries, the poor are employed to cultivate the land, but for the rest, there is almost no analogy between the two systems.

NOTES

Introduction

1. The Poor Law Amendment Act changed poverty relief in England and Wales; similar reforms were made to Scottish poverty relief in 1845.

2. At the time of their inception, the poor laws were widely regarded as a sign of England's moral and financial greatness: her ability to make charity a national political principle.

3. One drawback to this system was that relief was provided only to residents of a parish. The Settlement Act of 1662 allowed paupers who could not prove "settlement" (residency) in a parish or who could not find work in forty days to be removed from a parish. Adam Smith criticized the restrictions this placed on workers' freedom of movement in *Wealth of Nations* (1.10.c).

4. Edmund Burke's "Thoughts and Details on Scarcity" is his critical response to these flaws in the Speenhamland System.

5. Gertrude Himmelfarb, introduction to *Memoir on Pauperism*, by Alexis de Tocqueville, trans. Seymour Drescher (London: IEA Health and Welfare Unit, 1997), 6; Karl Polanyi, *The Great Transformation: The Political and Economic Origins of Our Time* (Boston: Beacon Press, 1957; first published 1944), 80.

6. See Tocqueville, *Democracy in America*, introduction to vol. 1. All references to *Democracy in America* are to the historical-critical edition, edited by Eduardo Nolla and translated by James T. Schleifer (Indianapolis: Liberty Fund, 2010).

7. In this context, lords and peasants, but a similar hierarchy also existed between kings and lords.

8. See Tocqueville's discussions of the democratic propensity for change and improvement, as well as how the constant agitation of American society leads to innovation and commercial greatness (*Democracy in America*, 338, 643). Yet this perpetual agitation can also be enervating and overwhelming, causing people to "prefer the social paralysis given by despotism to the great emotions of liberty" (1251).

9. Tocqueville, *Memoir*, 45. Hereafter, works by Tocqueville will omit reference to his name.

10. *Democracy in America*, 571.

11. See *Memoir*, 11, in this volume.

12. *Memoir*, 12. The distinction is reminiscent of *Democracy in America*'s distinction between egoism and self-interest (882).

13. *Memoir*, 12.

14. *Democracy in America*, 389.

15. *Memoir*, 18.

16. This is another Rousseauian element to Tocqueville's thought.

17. "Pauperism in America," 53.

18. *Democracy in America*, 499. On the influence of laws upon mores, the draft of *Democracy in America* includes the following passage: "Laws, however, work toward producing the spirit, the mores, and the character of the people."

19. In *Democracy in America*, Tocqueville stresses the importance of local institutions and local liberties, saying, "Town institutions are to liberty what primary schools are to knowledge; they put it within the grasp of the people; they give them a taste of its peaceful practice and accustom them to its use" (102). He also hails administrative decentralization as a key method of preserving the kinds of citizen strength and vigor requisite for self-government (147).

20. *Memoir*, 17.

21. *Memoir*, 18.

22. *Memoir*, 19.

23. *Memoir*, 19. At the time of its passage, MP Daniel O'Conner's complaint that the Poor Law Amendment Act "did away with personal feelings and connections" strikes this same note.

24. *Democracy in America*, 914. See also *Democracy in America*, vol. 1 (1835), part 2, chapter 4, and vol. 2 (1840), part 2, chapter 7.

25. These are passing discussions in the *Memoir*. No details explaining what constitutes an emergency situation are given, nor does Tocqueville offer any account of the public education's purposes, scope, or curriculum.

26. See the discussion of this exposure on pp. xvi–xvii, above (under "The *Memoir on Pauperism*: A Tale of Three Paradoxes"), again keeping in mind that Tocqueville seems not to recognize the market's dynamism.

27. See p. xx–xxi, above (under "The Second Paradox").

28. *Second Memoir on Pauperism*, 31. These virtues are also among the bourgeois virtues.

29. Agricultural colonies, moreover, were possible only in countries like the United States, with vast quantities of unoccupied, fertile lands that could be sold by the state to the poor at reduced prices. The uniqueness of the United States in this regard is likely why Tocqueville does not develop this idea as a solution in the context of either France or England.

30. See p. xxiv, above. Recall, also, that Tocqueville defines "voluntary association" very broadly, including not only private associations but also a variety of associations established by law.

31. Whether this is or is not inevitable is debatable, Tocqueville's own views notwithstanding.

32. *Democracy in America*, 901.

33. Indeed, it is in the context of praising associative life that Tocqueville says, "The principle aim of good government has always been to make the citizens more and more able to do without its *help*. This is more useful than the help can be" (*Democracy in America*, 904).

34. *Democracy in America*, 898.

35. For Tocqueville, individualism always threatens to cause isolation and withdrawal into the circle of one's own family and friends. Among other concerns, he fears that this retreat from the public sphere will facilitate soft despotism.

36. *Democracy in America*, 893.

37. Ibid., 900.

38. Ibid., 160.

Memoir on Pauperism (1835)

1. Tocqueville delivered this address to the Royal Academic Society of Cherbourg in 1835, and it was published in the *Mémoires de la société académique de Cherbourg* (1835), 293–344.

2. The French term is *commune* (here in the plural, *communes*), traditionally translated in *Democracy in America* as "township." For

Tocqueville, this is the basic unit of governance and an essential element within a free democracy. In the township, individuals learn the art of political and voluntary association, as well as how to exercise self-interest well understood. All of these are essential elements for a free democratic society.

3. Alban de Villeneuve-Bargemont (1784–1850) was a French political figure and economist whose thoughts about the causes of and solutions to modern poverty influenced Tocqueville. The figure cited would have been drawn from Villeneuve-Bargemont's *Économie politique chrétienne, ou recherches sur la nature et les causes du paupérisme en France et en Europe et sur les moyens de le soulager et de le prévenir* (1834).

4. Albiano Balbi (1782–1848) was a well-known Italian geographer. His *Essai statistique sur le royaume de Portugal et d'Algarve* (1822) is the most likely source of the statistic.

5. The department of the Nord is North, in the Pas-de-Calais region; the Creuse is in South-Central France, in the former region of Limousin (now Nouvelle-Aquitaine); the Manche is to the North, in Lower Normandie.

6. The French is *sauvage*, which can mean "savage," but also "wild" or "natural."

7. The French is *esprit*, which can mean both "mind" and "spirit."

8. Mores (*moeurs*) are another central Tocquevillian concept that is difficult to translate into English. Often translated as "manners" or "morals," and sometimes shorthanded as "habits of the heart," the term *mores* encompasses the entire set of beliefs, ideas, opinions, manners, morals, and habits of a people. In *Democracy in America*, Tocqueville asserts that mores are by far the most important factor in preserving liberty and that when mores and laws conflict, it is law that will give way. Significantly, Tocqueville also believes that women are the guardians of mores.

9. Representing the largest portion of the nation, the *tiers état* was, together with the nobility and the clergy, one of the three orders into which the prerevolutionary French nation was divided within the Estates-General.

10. The secretary of the Royal Academic Society of Cherbourg was Joseph Laurent Couppey, a civil tribunal judge who published various studies about Normandy in the Middle Ages.

11. The French is *de son industrie* and could also connote involvement in trade or manufacturing.

12. The French is *misérable*; *la misère* is poverty.

13. The ellipsis points are Tocqueville's.

14. *Sauvage*, or uncivilized.

15. The office of overseer of the poor existed from 1597 until 1834. Each parish was required to have two overseers, who were elected annually and who were responsible for administering poor relief and for determining who was—or was not—a fitting recipient of relief.

16. While I have chosen "village" as the appropriate translation for *commune* in discussions pertaining to England, I have followed most translators in using "township" for *commune* in Tocqueville's discussions of France and the United States.

17. The French is *inquiétude*, which is one of the central characteristics of the democratic soul Tocqueville describes in the 1840 volume of *Democracy in America*.

18. The French is *un pauvre*, which I have here translated as "pauper," for Tocqueville's point is that this apparently prosperous individual is a claimant of legal charity.

19. Tocqueville uses *l'administrateur des pauvres*. Elsewhere I have translated *administrateur* as "administrator," but here I have translated Tocqueville's phrase as "overseer of the poor," since overseers' judgments were appealed to justices of the peace, as in this case.

20. The French is *égoïste*. In *Democracy in America*, Tocqueville contrasts egoism with individualism. He characterizes the former as the passionate and exaggerated type of self-love that has always existed, and he contrasts it with individualism, which is a rational sentiment that originates in democratic times and that leads the individual to turn away from public life.

21. Its vibrant associative life was one of the things that most struck Tocqueville about the United States. Within a democracy, associations took the place of the powerful individuals found in aristocracies. The science of association, he thought, was "the mother science" and essential to the preservation of democratic liberty. Associative life's positive psychological effects included tempering isolated individualism and augmenting the individual's sense of his/her own strength; both of these, thought Tocqueville, were important safeguards against soft despotism.

Second Memoir on Pauperism (1837)

1. Substitutions, abolished in 1792, allowed the undivided transmission of landed property from generation to generation.

2. In "Advice to a Young Tradesman, Written by an Old One" (1748), Franklin writes, "In short, the Way to Wealth, if you desire it, is as plain as the Way to Market. It depends chiefly on two Words, Industry and Frugality; i.e. Waste neither Time nor Money, but make the best Use of both." See Ralph L. Ketcham, ed., *The Political Thought of Benjamin Franklin* (Indianapolis: Hackett, 2003), 53.

3. The word is *éclairés*, which can also mean "knowledgeable."

4. A word is missing in the text.

5. The term gains an exploitative connotation through Marx and Engels, writing after Tocqueville.

6. Tocqueville notes that by "England," he means "that portion of the British Isles that includes England properly speaking, Wales, and Ireland."

7. The ellipsis points are Tocqueville's. Perhaps he intended to develop the point further.

8. Tocqueville plays upon the sense of *fortune* as destiny and its economic sense.

9. In contributing money to saving banks, the poor would be "loaning" money to the state, which the state might misuse ("seize"). But it would also be possible that all of the poor would suddenly—"by their own imprudence"—have need of their deposits, in which case there would be a run on the savings banks. If everyone tried to withdraw, the State (which Tocqueville here calls the "creditor" of the poor lenders) would not have sufficient funds to pay out, and it would "go bankrupt."

10. That is, political or economic crisis.

11. Charles Dupin (1784–1873) was a French mathematician and economist. His works in political economy focus on both Britain and France.

12. The phrase is *le fait générateur*; Tocqueville deploys the same term in the opening paragraphs of *Democracy in America*, describing equality of conditions he observes in the United States.

13. The word is *lumière*, which can also mean "knowledge."

14. In the margin, Tocqueville had jotted, "In sum, the public treasury gives the poor all the advantages of a state-backed asset, and it undertakes all of the risks."

15. *Un recours*, or the legal right to demand payment or compensation.

16. Begun in northern Italy in the fifteenth century, the *monts-de-piété* (mounts of piety; sometimes also called Lombard Banks) were early charitable organizations run by the Catholic Church that made loans to needy individuals at moderate interest rates. Borrowers deposited items of value in exchange for a monetary loan of part of the item's value; the interest from the loan paid the *mont-de-piété*'s operating expenses. The capital to be lent was donated by individuals and corporations who contributed to the *mont-de-piété* as a charity rather than an investment. Because *monts-de-piété* were independently run by towns, interest rates varied. At the beginning of the nineteenth century, the rate of the Paris *monts-de-piété* would have exceeded 30 percent, though by the time Tocqueville was writing, that rate had fallen to about 7 percent. Thus, the 12 percent Tocqueville mentions is at the high end of the national spectrum, though his calling that rate "highly usurious" should also be understood in a context in which private moneylenders might have charged more than 40 percent interest.

17. *Hospices*, where the elderly and poor could be housed and cared for.

18. Here, Tocqueville uses *hôpitaux*, whose meaning at the time was interchangeable with "hospice."

19. In the margin, Tocqueville jots, "This would be a veritable bank of the poor, for which the poor would furnish the funds." These reformed savings associations would be hybrid entities, combining the state-sponsored savings bank with the private *monts-de-piété*.

20. Throughout these paragraphs, the French is *administration*.

21. A word is missing in the text.

22. In the 1830s, Félix de Viville, who was the first to hold simultaneous directorships of both the *mont-de-piété* and the savings bank in Metz, authored several pamphlets on savings banks and *monts-de-piété*.

23. A word is missing in the text.

Letter on Pauperism in Normandy

1. The surviving fragment of this unfinished letter begins midsentence, midthought. Neither the intended recipient nor the date of the letter fragment is known. The use of the familiar "you" (*tu*) indicates that it was probably a relative, perhaps Tocqueville's brother, Hippolyte.

2. The text here contains the following marginal note: "Next, the ease of returning all of the poor citizens. Public minister who speaks to the township in order to know."

3. In the margin, Tocqueville commented, "This would be a kind of mutual insurance against begging."

4. A note in the margin here reads, "It would even be possible to establish real savings banks for the rural poor. Idea to examine."

5. Tocqueville's marginal note reads, "While serving as public minister, I noticed that more than half of the thieves had been beggars in their childhoods."

6. The [?] is Tocqueville's. The individual's identity is unknown.

7. Tocqueville's brother, Édouard de Tocqueville.

Pauperism in America (1833)

1. The French is *droit*, which also means "right."

2. Emphasis added.

3. *Communes*. See *Memoir on Pauperism*, n. 2, in the present volume.

4. Maryland's Laws of 1768 contained provisions for state-supported almshouses, or charitable houses.

5. Expenditures for poor relief reached their height in the 1818–20 period, when they were approximately 8.75 million pounds per year and 2.7 percent of annual gross domestic product.

6. Tocqueville uses the English here.

7. Small farming outposts. *Colonies agricoles* were rural outlets for the urban underclass, established with the hope that agricultural life would allow the individual to become materially self-sufficient, while also teaching him/her the so-called agrarian virtues, including the work ethic, order, patience, steadfastness, etc.

INDEX

Catholic Church, 63n16
centralization
　in America, 55na
　economic dangers of, 39–40
　in public charity, xxii
　and savings banks, 39–40
　tendencies toward, in democra-
　　cies, xxix
　Tocqueville's opposition to, xxii,
　　xxviii–xxix, 58n19
　See also government
children
　and illegitimacy concerns,
　　xxi–xxii, 20, 24–25
　schools for, xxv, xxxi, 26, 58n25
　subsidies for, xiv, 24–25
Christianity, 12
Church of England, xiii, 12–13
comforts
　during feudalism, 6–7, 8
　impact of industrialism on, 8–9
　in psychology of desire,
　　xvii–xviii
　See also desires
Couppey, Joseph Laurent, 5,
　60n10
Creuse department (France), 2,
　60n5
criminality
　impact of voluntary associations
　　on, 49–50
　links between pauperism and,
　　xii, 20
　as unintended consequence of
　　public charity, xxi

decentralization, xxviii–xxix,
　58n19. *See also* government;
　local governance and action

democracies
　dangers of individualism in,
　　59n35, 61n20
　decentralization needed in,
　　xxviii–xxix, 58n19
　distinctiveness of Tocqueville's
　　analysis of, xi–xii
　dynamic economy in, xvi–xvii
　generating feelings of weakness
　　and isolation, xxix, xxxi
　as inevitable future, xii
　perpetual change and innovation
　　in, 58n8
　psychology of equality in,
　　xvii–xviii
　role of local governance to, xxii,
　　xxviii–xxix, 58n19, 59n2
　role of voluntary associations in,
　　xii, xxiv–xxv, xxviii–xxix, 36,
　　59n2, 61n21
　soft despotism in, xxix, xxx–
　　xxxi, 58n8
　tendencies toward centralization
　　in, xxix
Democracy in America
　(Tocqueville)
　continuities with *Memoir on
　　Pauperism*, xii
　contrasting egoism with indi-
　　vidualism, 58n12, 61n20
　on democratic soul character-
　　istics, 61n17
　on economic dynamism,
　　xvi–xvii, 59n26
　ending warning of dangers,
　　xxxii
　on equality, xv, xvii
　impact of *Penitentiary Report*
　　on, xii

on importance of voluntary
associations, xii, xxxiii, 58n19
on local action and governance,
xii, 58n19
on local political participation
countering individualism,
xxxii–xxxiii
psychology in, xii
relation between laws and mores
in, 58n18
rights praised in, xix
on role of mores in preserving
liberty, 60n8
on soft despotism, xxix
Tocqueville remembered for, xi
on voluntary associations–
government relationship, xxix
desires
during feudalism, 6–7
impact of industrialism on, 8–9
psychology of, xvii–xviii, 10–11
in stages of societal development, 3–7
turning into needs, xv–xviii,
7–11
despotism. See soft despotism
Discourse on the Origin of
Inequality (Rousseau), xv
Drescher, Seymour, xxix
Dupin, Charles, 41, 62n11

economy
dangers of centralization in,
39–40
dynamism of, xvi–xvii, 59n26
static views of, xvi–xvii
uncertainties in modern, xxvii
education, xxv, xxxi, 26, 58n25
egoism, 58n12, 61n20

Elizabeth I (queen of England),
xiii, 13, 25
England
consolidation of farming in, 14,
30–31
history of poor relief in, xiii–xiv,
12–13
industrialism in, 13–14, 34–35
land ownership in, 14, 32
paradox of pauperism in
wealthiest country, xv–xviii,
1–2, 10–11
principle of legal charity in,
12–22, 57n2
rates of pauperism in, xv, 2, 17
savings banks in, 37, 41
taxes for poor relief in, xiii, 13,
53
Tocqueville's definition of, 62n6
Tocqueville's travels through, xi,
22–25
wealth of, 1–2, 11, 57n2
See also poor laws (England)
equality
in Democracy in America, xv,
xvii
in democratic societies, xvii–xviii
in French property ownership, 30
impact on pauperism, xvii–xviii,
xxix–xxx
in rights, 18
tension between liberty and,
xxviii–xxix, xxxiv
in Tocqueville's account of
societal development, 5

feudalism
compared to industrialism, 33
ending of, xv

feudalism (*cont.*)
  hierarchical relationships in, xv,
    57n7
  inequalities of, xv–xvi, 5–7
  in Tocqueville's account of
    societal development, 5–7
France
  agricultural classes in, xxv–xxvi,
    32
  analyzed in *The Old Regime
    and the Revolution*, xi
  bankruptcies declared by
    government in, 40
  industrial classes in, xxvi, 14nc,
    32–35
  property ownership in, xxvi–
    xxvii, 30, 32, 41–42, 62n1
  rates of pauperism in, 2, 55nb
  savings banks in, xxviii, 37–42
  social orders in prerevolu-
    tionary, 60n9
  substitutions abolished in, 30,
    32, 62n1
  taxation in, 37, 38
  voluntary association examples
    in, 50
Franklin, Benjamin, 31
  "Advice to a Young Tradesman,"
    62n2

goods (nonessential)
  of aristocracy, xv–xvii, 6–7
  dynamism in markets of,
    xvi–xvii
  and equality, xvi, xvii–xviii,
    6–7
  in psychology of desire, 10–11
  risks in production of, xvi, xxxiv,
    8–9
  See also industrialism

government
  in America, 52, 55na
  bankruptcies in French govern-
    ments, 40
  dangers of soft despotism, xxx–
    xxxi, xxxii, xxxiii
  and decentralization, xxviii–xxix,
    58n19
  goals of good government,
    59n33
  relation to voluntary associ-
    ations, 36, 47
  role in civic renewal, xxxiii,
    58n19
  role in public charity adminis-
    tration, xiii–xiv, xxxi–xxxii,
    12–13, 52
  role in savings bank administra-
    tion, 37–41, 45–46, 62n9,
    62n14
  in Tocqueville's account of
    society's development, 4–5
  See also centralization; local
    governance and action

Henry VIII (king of England), xiii,
  12
Himmelfarb, Gertrude, xiv
Holland, 56nd

idleness
  habits of, 52, 54
  impact of right to charity on,
    xx–xxi, 15, 17, 19–20, 27
  as natural human trait, xx, 3, 15
illegitimacy
  destigmatization of, xxi–xxii,
    24–25
  increases in, 20, 25
  and subsidies, xiv

individualism
  egoism contrasted with, 58n12,
    61n20
  impacts on democracy, 59n35,
    61n20
  isolation and withdrawal caused
    by, 59n35
  local political participation
    countering, xxxii–xxxiii
  voluntary associations coun-
    tering, xxiv–xxv, 61n21
industrialism
  agricultural workers moving to,
    xv–xvi, 7–8, 9, 13–14, 30–31
  challenges presented by, 28
  commercial crises in, 33–35
  elements of feudalism seen in,
    33
  in England, 13–14, 34–35
  in France, 14nc, 32–35
  impact of farming consolidation
    on, 14, 30–31
  impact of foreign markets on,
    34–35
  impact on desires and needs, 8–9
  including trade and manu-
    facturing, 61n11
  increased pauperism due to,
    xv–xvi, 8–9, 13–14
  paupers among industrial
    classes, 29, 30–31, 32–34
  personal savings of paupers
    working in, 36–46
  property ownership through
    factory shares in, xxvi–xxvii,
    33, 35–36
  risks and insecurities of, xvi,
    xxvi, xxix, xxxiii–xxxiv, 8–9,
    13, 32–35
  social impacts of, xxix, xxx

solutions to pauperism among,
    xxvi–xxvii, 35–46
  in Tocqueville's societal develop-
    ment stages, 7–9
  workers' associations in, xxxi,
    36
inequality
  during feudalism, xv–xvi, 5–7
  in Rousseau's *Discourse on the
    Origin of Inequality*, xv
  in Tocqueville's stages of societal
    development, 4–7
  See also equality
Ireland, 62n6
Italy, xxviii, 63n16

land ownership
  consolidation of, 14, 30–31
  economic empowerment
    through, xxxiii–xxxiv, 31–32
  in England, 14, 32
  in France, 30, 32, 41–42, 62n1
  as goal of savings, 41–42
  impacts on mores and habits,
    xxvi–xxvii, 31–32
  as solution to poor of agricul-
    tural classes, xxvi–xxvii,
    xxxiii–xxxiv, 29–32, 41–42
  substitutions, 30, 32, 62n1
  in Tocqueville's stages of societal
    development, 3–6
laws and legislation
  against begging, 50
  inability to reinvigorate citizen
    initiative, xxxiii
  on public charity in America,
    51–55, 64n4 ("Pauperism in
    America")
  regarding land ownership, 32
  regarding savings banks, 38, 41

Poor Law Relief Act (1601), xiii,
13, 57n3
poor laws (England)
administrative overseers of, xiii,
xiv, 13, 16–17
artificially lowering wages, xiv
categories of poor under, xiii,
16
enactment of, xiii, 13
examples of abuses produced by,
22–25
funding of, xiii, 13, 53
impact on mobility and liberty,
21, 57n3
impact on mores, 17–20, 22–25
impact on personal connections,
19, 58n23
impact on work ethic, xx–xxi,
15, 17, 19–20
increasing number of paupers
under, xii, xiv, 13, 20
reforms to, xi, xiii–xiv, xxii, 25,
57n1, 57n4, 58n23
role of the state in, xiii–xiv
as sign of moral and financial
greatness, 57n2
Speenhamland System, xiii–xiv,
57n4
unintended consequences of, xiv,
14–27, 57n3, 58n23
work conditions under, xiii, xiv,
13, 15–17
poor relief
historical background of, xiii–
xiv, 12–13
recommended amount of, 47
role of the government in, xxxiii
types of, xviii–xix, 12
as a virtue, 12, 26

See also private charity; public
charity
Portugal, 2
poverty. *See* pauperism; paupers
private charity
beginnings of, 12
benefits of, xxiii, xxiv–xxv, 12,
26, 27–28
church-administered, xiii, 12–13,
63n16
compared to public charity,
xviii–xix, xxiii–xxv, 12, 17,
18–19, 26–28
connections built through, xxiv–
xxv, 19
hybrid savings bank system as,
xxvii–xxviii, 43–46, 63n19
individual private charity, xviii,
xxiii, xxvii, 12, 26, 27–28,
48–49
mont-de-piété as form of, 63n16
as a natural impulse, xviii
pauper's inferior status in, 18–19
provided by aristocracy, xxx
through voluntary associations,
xxxi–xxxii, 47–50
weaknesses of, xxiii, xxvii, 26,
27–28, 48–49
property ownership
in England, 14, 32
through factory shares, 35–36
in France, xxvi, 30, 32, 41–42,
62n1
impact on mores, xxvi–xxvii,
31–32
impact on risks and insecurities,
xxvi, xxxiii–xxxiv, 32
in the industrial classes, 33
through personal savings, 36–46

taxation
  in America, 52, 56
  in England, xiii, 13, 53
  in France, 37, 38
  resentment created through,
    xxiii, xxiv
Tocqueville, Alexis de
  distinctive analysis of, xi–xii
  influences on, xi–xii, xv, xvii,
    58n16, 60n3
  travels to England, xi, 22–25
  travels to the United States, xii
Tocqueville, Édouard de, 50, 64n7
  ("Letter on Pauperism in
    Normandy")
Tocqueville, Hippolyte de, 63n1

unions, xxxi, 36
United States of America
  agricultural colonies to support
    the poor in, xxvii, 56, 59n29,
    64n7 ("Pauperism in
    America")
  associative life in, 61n21
  centralization of government in,
    55na
  dynamic economy in, xvi–xvii
  expenditures for public charity
    in, 55–56, 64n5 ("Pauperism
    in America")
  influence of England on charity
    in, 51
  Maryland example, 52–53
  New York state charity figures,
    54–56
  overseers of public charity in,
    51–53, 54–55
  problems with public charity in,
    xxi, 52–54

public charity as a right in, 51
taxation in, 52, 56
Tocqueville's travels to, xii
work requirements in, 51–52, 56
See also *Democracy in America*

Villeneuve-Bargemont, Alban de,
  2, 60n3
Viville, Félix de, 63n22
voluntary associations
  advantages of, 48–50
  as approach to social problems,
    xxix, xxxiv, 59n33
  collective strength through,
    xxx–xxxi, 48–49
  connections supplied by, xxx,
    xxxii–xxxiii, 49
  countering individualism,
    xxiv–xxv, 61n21
  in democracies, xii, xxiv–xxv,
    xxviii–xxix, 36, 59n2, 61n21
  empowerment through, xxx
  goals of, 47
  impact on soft despotism, xxxi,
    xxxiii, 61n21
  Mareuil township example, 50
  membership in, 48–49
  organization and governance of,
    47–50
  providing charity through, xxix,
    xxx, 47–50
  reformed savings banks as a
    form of, xxviii
  relation to government, xxxiii,
    47
  Tocqueville's definition of,
    59n30
  workers' industrial associations,
    xxxi, 36

CHRISTINE DUNN HENDERSON
is associate professor of political science in the School of
Social Sciences at Singapore Management University. She has
published extensively on Tocqueville as well as on politics and
literature, and she is the editor and translator of several books,
including *Tocqueville's Voyages*.

CPSIA information can be obtained
at www.ICGtesting.com
Printed in the USA
BVHW040226110121
597531BV00020B/1127

9 780268 109059